YORK

General Editors
of Stirling) & P
University of Be

Robert Browning

MEN AND WOMEN

Notes by Mary Montaut

MA (CAMBRIDGE) PH D (LONDON)
Tutor in English, University College, Dublin

LONGMAN
YORK PRESS

YORK PRESS
Immeuble Esseily, Place Riad Solh, Beirut.

LONGMAN GROUP LIMITED
Longman House,
Burnt Mill,
Harlow,
Essex.

First published 1984
ISBN 0 582 79251 7

Printed in Hong Kong by
Wilture Printing Co Ltd.

Contents

Part 1

Introduction

The life and works of Robert Browning

Robert Browning was born on 7 May 1812, in Camberwell, just south-
east of London. Today Camberwell is indistinguishable from the rest of
the great metropolis, but in Browning's childhood there were meadows,
woods and pleasant fresh air to stroll in. His father was a clerk in the
Bank of England and, though the family was comfortably off, they were
never rich. In spite of this, Browning's father had a passion for books
and was able to provide an exceptionally extensive library for his son to
browse through. In his early years, Browning read Francis Quarles's
book of *Emblems* (in an illustrated edition of 1777 which he later
described as the 'pet book of my childhood'); several old encyclopaedic
books such as Nathaniel Wanley's *Wonders of the Little World* (1678)
which is a collection of the most curious and bizarre 'facts', recorded
with unquestioning seriousness; and the fifty volumes of *Biographie
Universelle* (1822) where he first read about many of the historical
personages who inhabit his poems; Jeremy Collier's *Great Historical
Geographical, Genealogical, and Poetical Dictionary* (1701–21); and Dr
Johnson's *Dictionary* (1755) which is the source of many of the more
difficult words which Browning uses. Books such as these provided the
basis of the most eclectic education imaginable, and they reflect the
wide-ranging tastes of his father, the 'living encyclopaedia' as a relative
jokingly called him.

Browning's father was a remarkable man. He was the son of a banker
who owned a sugar plantation in St Kitt's in the West Indies. Browning's
father was sent out there to manage this planatation, but he was so
horrified and disgusted by the system of slavery that he came back to
England against his father's orders, was disowned by him and so took up
the position as clerk in the Bank of England which he held until he
retired in 1852. In a letter to Elizabeth Barrett, dated 26 August 1846,
Browning says:

> My father on his return had the intention of devoting himself to art,
> for which he had many qualifications and abundant love – but the
> quarrel with his father – who married again and continued to hate
> him till a few years before his death – induced him to go at once and
> consume his life after a fashion he always detested.

It is easy to imagine that, after such an experience, Browning's father was determined that his son should not be forced to do anything against his will. He was a great lover of painting, as well as books, and he probably hoped that Robert would become a painter as he had been frustrated in this ambition himself, although he never tried to force it upon his son. He used to take him to the near-by Picture Gallery at Dulwich College, and to let him read his books on painting. One of these books, Gérard de Lairesse's* *The History of Painting in All its Branches* (1707), was a special favourite with the boy and its influence on him was so profound that when he was seventy-five he wrote a poem about it called 'Parleying with Gérard de Lairesse' (1887). There is no doubt that Browning was strongly influenced by his father's tastes at this early stage of his life, and this influence continued to a greater or lesser degree throughout his life. His father was especially fond of Dutch genre painting (pictures of ordinary life) and of the work of William Hogarth (1697–1764). He was a fine caricaturist himself, and spent hours entertaining his own and other people's children with his comical 'lightning sketches'. Browning's own drawings are very similar to his father's, and quite astute psychologically.

This influence of the older Browning goes even deeper than this. His taste in literature was for the eighteenth-century writers in English such as Alexander Pope (1688–1744) or Tobias Smollett (1721–71), and for the classics, especially the sixth-century BC Greek lyrical poet, Anacreon, and the Latin satirist Horace (65–8 BC). Some of the anti-romantic tendencies in Browning's poetry reflect this influence. His father introduced him to the classics in the most charming way, recalled by Browning in 'Development' (1887):

> My father was a scholar and knew Greek.
> When I was five years old, I asked him once
> 'What do you read about?'
> > 'The siege of Troy.'
> 'What is a siege, and what is Troy?'
> > > Whereat
> He piled up chairs and tables for a town,
> Set me a-top for Priam, called our cat
> Helen . . . .

It is no surprise that Browning found ordinary school very dull after this lively and enthusiastic teaching at home. It is true to say that his real education took place at home, where he was free to read any book he liked and where he had a learned but entertaining companion with whom to discuss them all. Browning did not, however, meekly follow his

---

* De Lairesse (1641–1711) was a Dutch painter who wrote on art after he became blind.

father's tastes. As a boy, he was a great admirer first of Lord Byron (1788–1824) and then of Percy Bysshe Shelley (1792–1822), whereas the Romantic poets left his father cold. In later life, Browning said that he could not recall a time when he did not write verse. When he was twelve years old, he produced a volume of Byronic poems which his mother was keen to have published. She was a very musical woman, and Browning's lifelong love of music, as well as his thorough grounding in its theory and practice, is due to her. When he was fourteen, Browning was given a book of Shelley's poems which swept him off his feet. He not only loved them as poetry, he imitated Shelley's ideas. He must have made his respectable mother very anxious when he suddenly became an atheist and a vegetarian! This phase only lasted a couple of years, but his earliest long poem, *Pauline* (1833), displays the influence of Shelley's poetry and ideas.

In religion, Browning's family were Dissenters, that is to say, they did not belong to the Established Church of England. (Thomas Carlyle described a Dissenter as one who belonged to 'a free Church, making no noise'.) This meant that Browning could attend neither the University of Oxford nor that of Cambridge, but his father had ensured that he would be able to attend college if he wished by becoming a founding contributor to the establishment of University College, London. This college was specifically set up to cater for all religious denominations. Browning was one of its first students when the college opened in 1828, but he was not happy there and left in less than a year. It is easy to imagine how narrow and dull an academic approach to learning would seem to him, after the freedom of his father's library. He was also unhappy to be away from home, and there was no pressure put on him by his father to remain at University College if it did not suit him. The older man was happy to support his son as long as he liked. So Browning moved back home and continued to write and read, and prepare himself for a grand future, as he ironically described it later:*

> a foolish plan which occupied me mightily for a time and which had for its object the enabling me to assume and realise I know not how many different characters; – meanwhile the world was never to guess that 'Brown, Smith, Jones & Robinson' (as the spelling books have it) the respective authors of this poem, the other novel, such an opera, such a speech etc. etc. were no other than one and the same individual . . .

In his early twenties, Browning was clearly uncertain what kind of career to follow. He even attended lectures on physiology, not as a training but more out of his general interest in knowledge. He had a

* In a note on the fourth page of a copy of *Pauline* (1833) which he gave to John Forster in 1837.

human skull on his writing desk at home, more, it would seem, in a scientific than a philosophic or romantic spirit. In 1834 he became a diplomatic secretary to the Russian consul-general in London and accompanied him on a three-month tour of Russia, but he did not pursue a diplomatic career either. During the same year, he began his long poems, *Paracelsus* and *Sordello*, and contributed to the magazine of a 'set' of young men called the Colloquials, aspiring writers, lawyers, academics, painters and so on. The Colloquials were also enthusiastic theatre-goers. Besides this, Browning would go over to Paris and stay with one of his father's brothers who worked for Rothschilds, the bankers, there; this uncle was a 'linguist, antiquary and prodigious amateur scholar', a bit like Browning's father. With such a diverting existence, it is perhaps surprising that he wrote any poetry at all! However, he published *Paracelsus* in 1835 and it was favourably received. One of the people it impressed deeply was a woman poet called Elizabeth Barrett who felt 'the pulse of poetry is full and warm and strong in it . . . the author is a poet in the holy sense' (Letter to Mary Russell Mitford, July or August 1836). The publication of *Paracelsus* was paid for by Browning's devoted father.

Through the moderate success of this poem, Browning met the young but already influential critic, Dickens's biographer John Forster (1812–76), who introduced him to the most famous actor-manager of the day, William Macready (1793–1873). In a flush of gracious enthusiasm, Macready invited Browning to write a play for him, and this fired his first really firm ambition. He wrote a play called *Strafford* in 1836 which Macready performed with some success in spite of his gloomy forebodings. If Browning resented the amount of interference which Macready thought himself entitled to make, he did not show it at this stage and continued to write plays for him which were more or less rejected, either outright or by neglect.

None the less, the experience of playwriting must have determined Browning to be a dramatic poet, and he took his first trip to Italy in 1838 to gather material for his poem, *Sordello*, which ultimately took him seven years to complete. The publication of this monstrous poem in 1840 undid much of the reputation which Browning had built up. Macready's comment in his diary is, 'I yield to the belief that he will *never write again* – to any purpose. I fear his intellect is not quite clear.' But if *Sordello* cost him some admirers, it also gained him some who were very discriminating. Dante Gabriel Rossetti (1828–82), the poet and painter, had already admired Browning's poems, but he was delighted by *Sordello* and used to read it aloud to his fellow painters as they worked. Another product of Browning's trip to Italy was *Pippa Passes* (1841), which is neither a play nor a poem but an intensely original hybrid between the two forms.

At this stage of his life, Browning was energetic, sociable, talkative and just a little bit dandified. He had continued to write shorter poems and in 1842 he published a collection called *Dramatic Lyrics*, as well as another play, *King Victor and King Charles*. Even in this first collection of poems, the diversity of subject-matter and tone of voice is striking, and the collection has a predominantly comic, not a tragic, effect. Unfortunately all his plays, as well as *Sordello*, attempted tragedy. *Dramatic Lyrics* contained, for instance, 'My Last Duchess', 'Soliloquy of the Spanish Cloister', 'Johannes Agricola in Meditation' and 'Porphyria's Lover' which are some of Browning's finest dramatic monologues, as well as 'The Pied Piper of Hamelin' which he wrote to cheer up Macready's little son when he was ill. In 1843 Browning was badly let down by Macready, who pulled out of performing the main part in his play *A Blot in the 'Scutcheon*, but the play did attract the attention of the novelist Charles Dickens (1812–70), whose kind comments, however, were not relayed to Browning until many years later. In 1844 Browning took a second trip to Italy and travelled at a leisurely pace northwards from Naples and then back along the Rhine towards England. It was on this trip that Browning first read Elizabeth Barrett's *Poems* (1844) which made him fall in love with her; among them was a poem called 'Lady Geraldine's Courtship' where a generous reference is made to his own work:

> There, obedient to her praying, did I read aloud ...
> ... at times, a modern volume, Wordsworth's solemn-thoughted idyl,
> Howitt's verse-balled, or Tennyson's enchanted reverie,
> Or from Browning some 'Pomegranate',* which, if cut deep down the middle,
> Shows a heart within blood-tinctured, of a veined humanity ...

The reference is generous in the light of Miss Barrett's comments in her letters at this time about how difficult and mysterious she finds Browning's poetry, though she admires it too.

In January 1845 when he was back in England, Browning wrote his first letter to the recluse Miss Barrett in the following terms: 'I love your verses with all my heart, my dear Miss Barrett ... and I love you too ...' At this stage, Elizabeth Barrett had a far higher reputation as a poet than Browning and was a considerable scholar too, having translated the *Prometheus Bound* of the Greek tragedian Aeschylus (525–456 BC); it was published in 1833 when she was twenty-seven. She was very nearly forty by the time Browning met her, and six years his senior. Her letters give the impression of a lively and responsive woman, in spite of the fact that she was an invalid and almost never left her room. She met very few

---

* Browning published his poems and plays in a series called *Bells and Pomegranates*.

people face to face, though she had a large number of correspondents, and it was several months before she would allow Browning to visit her. He proposed to her soon afterwards, but she forbade him ever to speak of marriage to her again, knowing her father's tyrannical opposition to any of his children's marrying, and regarding herself as an invalid. Browning accepted this, and went on seeing her and writing to her without ever bringing up the subject until she let him. Their letters to each other during this period are, though love-letters, unembarrassing and interesting to read, as they argued and debated and discussed a great number of subjects, coming to understand each other thoroughly. In fact, if her doctor had not predicted that Elizabeth Barrett would not live through another English winter, or if her father had been generous enough to let her go to Italy with his permission, Browning might never have eloped with her. He finally did so, believing that she could die if she had to stay in England for another winter. By this time too, Elizabeth Barrett herself had realised the heartless quality in her adored father, who preferred to let her face death rather than allow her to go to Italy; and her acceptance of Browning and his love was total and grateful. They were secretly married on 12 September 1846, eloped five days later to Paris, and then went on to Italy.

In terms of Browning's career as a writer, this event disrupted whatever circle and reputation he had acquired, and for many years afterwards his published work was received with apathy in England and his contacts with the theatre collapsed. After the publication of two plays, *Luria* and *A Soul's Tragedy* in 1846, he only wrote the brief piece, 'In a Balcony' (in *Men and Women*, 1855), in true dramatic form, and during the first four years of his marriage he wrote very little poetry of any kind. During this time, the Brownings lived first at Pisa and then in Casa Guidi in Florence, which was their base for the next fourteen years, until Elizabeth died. In Florence, they were part of a very artistic community of English and Americans, including poets and painters, sculptors and antiquarians. In 1849 Elizabeth gave birth to a son and in that same year Browning published a collected edition of his works excluding *Sordello, Strafford* and *Pauline*. By this time he was working on a long religious poem called *Christmas Eve and Easter Day* (1850), which treats in a discursive and diffuse way several of the predominant themes which are more objectively and confidently explored in *Men and Women*. Elizabeth's influence is at its strongest in this poem and it is not entirely characteristic of Browning. Her effect was not intentional, however; the two poets always respected each other's work and the need for privacy in which to write, each believing that the other's work was the greater. They both became very interested in the cause of Italian freedom, but they disagreed over Elizabeth's faith in spiritualism. These themes occur in *Men and Women*.

Browning's long-held interest in painting increased in Italy and he studied Vasari's* *Lives of the Most Eminent Painters* and Baldinucci's† *Notes on the Artists* in great depth. He also scoured the street market in Florence for old pictures and bought some very fine ones. He was taught to sculpt by a close friend, the American sculptor William Wetmore Story (1819–95), and shared the education of his little son with Elizabeth, teaching him to play the piano and ride a horse. During this period, the Brownings made several trips to London and Paris as well as spending months in Rome. They were friendly with many of the Pre-Raphaelites‡, who were being championed in England by John Ruskin, and they also corresponded with him. One of Browning's closest friends was the painter, Frederick Leighton (1830–96), who later became the President of the Royal Academy in England, and Elizabeth Barrett Browning (EBB) shared her interest in spiritualism with Frederick Tennyson (1807–98), a minor poet and brother of Alfred, Lord Tennyson (1809–92). Perhaps the most illuminating of the friendships of this happy period of Browning's life, however, was with the old poet Walter Savage Landor (1775–1864), who had been cast off by his family. Browning more or less became his protector. EBB reported in her letters how tolerant Browning was of the old man's tempers and oddities, and mentioned that the old classicist was the poet 'to whom he owed more as a writer than to any contemporary'. The old Regency buck, who could remember Count Blessington d'Orsay (1801–52), the famous dandy, and who wrote beautifully turned Latin epigrams, was a man of Browning's father's generation and Georgian taste for classical elegance, wit and satire. Browning's understanding and admiration for him may have had something to do with his father's influence.

In 1861 EBB died suddenly, leaving Browning with his eleven-year-old son who was still wearing lacey collars and long curls. He put the boy into more manly clothes, had his hair cut, packed up everything in Casa Guidi and left Florence, unable to bear the place now that EBB was dead. He spent the first few months with his father and sister on the coast of Brittany, recovering from the blow of her loss, and then he moved to London with his son and began to work unremittingly on his poetry. He produced another collected edition in 1863 in which the poems of *Men and Women* were re-organised and only thirteen poems put under that title (see list on page 14), the rest being placed in *Dramatic Lyrics* and *Dramatic Romances*. In 1864 another splendid collection of poems was produced called *Dramatis Personae*, which included 'Mr Sludge, "the Medium"', 'James Lee's Wife', 'Abt Vogler' and 'Rabbi Ben Ezra'. Then

---

* Vasari (1512–74) was the first major biographer of the painters of the Italian Renaissance.
† Baldinucci (1624–96) was an art historian.
‡ The Pre-Raphaelite Brotherhood (1848) was a set of young revolutionary painters.

in 1868 Browning published his masterpiece, *The Ring and the Book*, one of the longest poems in English. From 1871 until his death in 1889, he continued to write copiously, both long poems and shorter pieces like those in *Men and Women*. In all these works, he maintained the convention of the dramatic monologue, which in fact became a way of protecting himself in his later years from prying critics, whom he detested. He trained his son to be a painter and died in his son's house in Venice on 12 December 1889, just a couple of days after the last collected edition of his works had been published in England.

Brief chronology of Browning's life

1812	Browning born. Dickens born. USA declares war on Britain
1815	Napoleon defeated at Waterloo
1821	Death of Keats
1822	Death of Shelley
1824	Death of Byron
1827	Tennyson publishes his first poems. Death of William Blake
1828	Browning briefly attends London University
1830	Louis Philippe elected King of France
1832	First Reform Bill passed in England
1833	Browning's first long poem, *Pauline*, published
1834	Browning's trip to Russia
1835	Browning's long poem, *Paracelsus*, published. Dickens's *Sketches by Boz* published
1837	Browning's first play, *Strafford*. Queen Victoria comes to the throne
1838	Browning's first vist to Italy.
1840	*Sordello* published. Queen Victoria marries Prince Albert
1841	*Pippa Passes* published
1844	Browning's second visit to Italy
1846	Browning marries Elizabeth Barrett and moves to Italy
1848	Revolutions in Italy
1849	Browning's son born in March. Browning's mother dies a few days later
1850	*Christmas Eve and Easter Day* published. Italian movement for unification
1855	*Men and Women* published. Tennyson's *Maud* published
1859	Darwin's *On the Origin of Species* published
1861	Death of EBB. Browning moves back to England. Death of Prince Albert
1864	*Dramatis Personae* published
1866	Death of Browning's father
1867	Second Reform Bill passed in England

1868   *The Ring and the Book* published

Browning continues to publish many long poems and collections

1889   December: Browning dies in Venice

A note on the text

Men and Women was first published in two volumes by Chapman & Hall, London, on 10 November 1855. These Notes have been based on the first volume of *Robert Browning: The Poems*, edited by John Pettigrew, supplemented and completed by Thomas J. Collins, Yale University Press, New Haven, Conn., and London, 1981, and Penguin Books, Harmondsworth, 1981.

Men and Women, 1855

The following list gives the contents of the 1855 publication. Browning's later redistribution of the poems for the collected edition of 1863 is shown in brackets after each title. (*DL* = *Dramatic Lyrics*; *DR* = *Dramatic Romances*; *M&W* = *Men and Women*.)

Volume I

1. Love Among the Ruins (*DL*)
2. A Lovers' Quarrel (*DL*)
3. Evelyn Hope (*DL*)
4. Up at a Villa – Down in the City (*DL*)
5. A Woman's Last Word (*DL*)
6. Fra Lippo Lippi (*M&W*)
7. A Toccata of Galuppi's (*DL*)
8. By the Fire-side (*DL*)
9. Any Wife to Any Husband (*DL*)
10. An Epistle of Karshish (*M&W*)
11. Mesmerism (*DR*)
12. A Serenade at the Villa (*DL*)
13. My Star (*DL*)
14. Instans Tyrranus (*DR*)
15. A Pretty Woman (*DL*)
16. 'Childe Roland to the Dark Tower Came' (*DR*)

17. Respectability (*DL*)
18. A Light Woman (*DR*)
19. The Statue and the Bust (*DR*)
20. Love in a Life (*DL*)
21. Life in a Love (*DL*)
22. How it Strikes a Contemporary (*M&W*)
23. The Last Ride Together (*DR*)
24. The Patriot: An Old Story (*DR*)
25. Master Hugues of Saxe-Gotha (*DL*)
26. Bishop Blougram's Apology (*M&W*)
27. Memorabilia (*DL*)

Volume II

28. Andrea del Sarto (*M&W*)
29. Before (*DL*)
30. After (*DL*)

31. In Three Days (*DL*)
32. In a Year (*DL*)
33. Old Pictures in Florence (*DL*)
34. In a Balcony (in *Tragedies and Other Plays* in 1863, then placed between *M&W* and *Dramatis Personae* in 1868)
35. Saul (*DL*)
36. 'De Gustibus –' (*DL*)
37. Women and Roses (*DL*)
38. Protus (*DR*)
39. Holy-Cross Day (*DR*)
40. The Guardian-Angel (*DL*)
41. Cleon (*M&W*)
42. The Twins (*DR*)
43. Popularity (*DL*)
44. The Heretic's Tragedy (*DR*)
45. Two in the Campagna (*DL*)
46. A Grammarian's Funeral (*DR*)
47. One Way of Love (*DR*)
48. Another Way of Love (*DL*)
49. 'Transcendentalism' (*M&W*)
50. Misconceptions (*DL*)
51. One Word More (*M&W*)

Men and Women, 1863

In the 1863 collected edition, the group *Men and Women* consisted of the eight poems indicated in the list above plus five additional poems. Details of the latter are given in brackets in the contents list below.

1. 'Transcendentalism'
2. How it Strikes a Contemporary
3. Artemis Prologizes (in *DL* 1842)
4. An Epistle of Karshish
5. Johannes Agricola in Meditation (first published in 1836)
6. Pictor Ignotus (in *DR* 1845)
7. Fra Lippo Lippi
8. Andrea del Sarto
9. The Bishop Orders his Tomb (first published in 1845)
10. Bishop Blougram's Apology
11. Cleon
12. Rudel to the Lady of Tripoli (in *DL* 1842)
13. One Word More

Part 2

Summaries

of MEN AND WOMEN

In the following summaries the poems are given in the order in which they appeared in the 1855 edition. For all the longer poems, line numbers are given in the Notes and Glossaries in brackets after the word or phrase being explained.

---

1. Love Among the Ruins

A pastoral scene is described by the speaker, who is strolling at evening to a tryst with his lover. His flocks are grazing on the grass which now completely conceals the ruins of an ancient city, and this observation gives rise to a series of reflections upon the contrast between the historical pomp of the scene and its present unassuming peacefulness. The speaker pictures the splendour and bustle of the past and the ambition of the ancient inhabitants for 'gold', and he contrasts this with the present. He enables the reader imaginatively to make the two pictures dissolve one into the other, producing ironic overtones. The speaker's easy frame of mind is accounted for by the confident expectation of his lover's adoring welcome awaiting him at the ruined turret, which is all that still stands of the city. He implies that her greeting can outweigh all the glory of the ancients: 'Love is best.'

NOTES AND GLOSSARY:
This poem takes a most unusual verse-form which ambles along, accompanying the speaker's thoughts. It is typically visual, even picturesque, in presentation, the essential thing being for the reader to visualise the descriptions and catch the fine distinctions, for example between the mistress's 'yellow' hair, and the 'gold' of the old city. The mood is relaxed, belonging to that phase of a love affair when the miracle is mutual trust. In such a mood, a shepherd could surely feel superior to the ancient kings whose very ruins are now almost lost.

 Browning altered the appearance of the stanzas in the 1863 edition by putting every pair of stanzas together to form one, making seven stanzas of twelve lines each. You will see that this alteration slightly enhances the effect of the contrast between the past and the present in the poem.

caper:	a small shrub
houseleek:	a small succulent plant (Latin *sempervivum*)
causeys:	causeways; mounds or dams made of stamped earth

2. A Lovers' Quarrel

The character of the speaker is really the subject of this poem, and so the reader needs to listen critically and in detail, however sympathetic he may be to the speaker's emotions, or else he may miss the point. Browning deliberately placed this poem to follow the confident mood of 'Love Among the Ruins'.

The speaker has spoiled an idyllic love affair by a spiteful word – or so he says. He describes the blissful winter with his mistress in contrast with the present rueful brightness of spring. The remarkable thing about his description of their pastimes is that it was all make-believe. His account of the quarrel is revealing; his spiteful word is called a 'shaft from the Devil's bow' (in contrast with Cupid's; Cupid is the Greek god of love whose arrows make people fall in love), but he never retracts it. He blames his mistress for over-reacting to the 'word', and believes she is wrong to hold it against him. With considerable self-pity he finds her alienation from him 'hard to bear', just as he found the springtime distasteful in the first stanza. He longs for winter, hoping his mistress will come back to his warmth; if she does, he will never let her go.

NOTES AND GLOSSARY:
The metre of this poem has a springy pace which cleverly undermines the speaker's self-pity and gives emphasis to his more attractive aspects of self-irony (like comparing himself to 'valiant Tom Thumb'). It is usual in Browning's poems about love to find the emotions are personal and complex, not ideal or vague, and these qualities here mean that it is impossible to judge what the quarrel was really about because the speaker is so plainly biased. The interest lies in the revelation of his character as he tries to justify himself.

I'd as lief that:	I'd rather that
rillets:	small streams or rivulets
beryl:	a precious stone, which can be greenish or amber
ingle:	hearth, fireplace
daws:	jackdaws
will our table turn?:	a reference to the spiritualist ritual for contacting the dead
lappet:	lapel of a coat
minor third:	the musical interval of the cuckoo's spring song
guelder-rose:	a snowball tree, with clusters of white flowers

3. Evelyn Hope

The speaker here, a man of about forty-eight, is addressing the corpse of a beautiful sixteen-year-old girl called Evelyn Hope. Her surname has an ironic connotation since the poem revolves around his hope of 'taking' her in the next life since he has missed her in this one. She never even knew him. None the less, he will not accept that they were nothing to each other, but believes that his love for her will be rewarded by God's giving her to him in heaven. On this presumption, he imagines how he will tell her that, in spite of his full and varied life since her death, he could not find satisfaction without her. The last line of stanza 6 is typical of Browning's way of using the character's own words to raise doubts about him: 'let us see' is decidedly ambivalent to the reader, though not to the speaker, providing a touch of dramatic irony. The speaker presses a leaf into the chilly hand of the dead girl, for he has so strongly physical an idea of the next life that he imagines her waking up, seeing the leaf, and remembering that she belongs to him. The whole poem is full of such confident expectations – and leaves the reader aghast at the speaker's presumption!

---

4. Up at a Villa – Down in the City

The 'Italian Person of Quality', as the speaker would doubtless like his hearer to consider him, describes his preference for city life by contrasting it with his life in a country villa. He likes company and events, the conveniences and entertainments of city life, but at the same time he is genuinely horrified at the cost of living in the city, and the reader may suspect that this would taint his enjoyment were his dream of living there realised. The imaginative picture which he draws of city life is, after all, free! Besides, his vivid description of the despised countryside around the villa shows that the speaker is observant of landscape even if he likes to parade his dislike of it, and this undermines his saying the country has 'nothing to see'. His description of the country moves at the pace of the seasons, whereas his vision of city-life is crammed with all its activities on one day. The substance of the poem is really the contrast between the two ways of life; the speaker's character, with its snobbishness and parsimony as well as its vivid imagination, provides a means of highlighting the contrast. The poem is humorous in tone, reflecting the speaker's jocose acceptance of his lot, and his discontent with rural life seems like an amusing pose. His lively imagination and gregariousness are attractive.

NOTES AND GLOSSARY:

Bacchus:	Greek god of wine
shag:	rough mass (of hair)
skull:	here the speaker scratches his own 'skull'
pash:	strike violently, dash something into pieces (here, water)
thrid:	thread

diligence:	a stage coach
Pulcinello:	Punch and Judy puppet show
the Duke's:	Duke Leopold II, Grand Duke of Tuscany
Dante:	Italian poet (1265–1321)
Boccaccio:	Italian story-writer (1313–75)
Petrarca:	Italian poet (1304–74)
Cicero:	Roman orator, writer and statesman (106–43 BC)
seven swords:	representing the seven sorrows of the Virgin Mary
new tax:	on salt and produce entering the city

5. A Woman's Last Word

This poem is a cleverly ambivalent expression of the woman's 'submission' at the end of a row with her lover. It is significant that she is taking the Last Word. Weariness with the quarrel is the main reason for ending it, but she is also frightened at the damage they are doing to their relationship in quarelling. Paradoxically, she claims that 'truth' must be 'false' because it makes her 'false to' her lover, which is a subtle way of continuing to assert that she is right. She compares herself to Eve, and the truth to the Apple in the Garden of Eden, and the very analogy lets us realise that her self-admonition not to take the apple will be of no avail – whatever her 'truth' is, we know that she won't relinquish it. She demands that her lover should be 'a god' or even 'a man' and protect her from that truth, replacing it with lessons in how to please him. She promises to give herself up to his teaching, but not yet – 'tomorrow'. Now she must weep until, exhausted, she falls asleep with him.

NOTES AND GLOSSARY:
It would be hard to miss the irony of this poem. Browning here displays his remarkable insight into the absurdity of expecting complete harmony even in very loving relationships; the speaker never doubts her lover loves her. She struggles to maintain her point of view with this.

serpent's tooth: Satan took the form of a serpent to tempt Eve

6. Fra Lippo Lippi

The poem opens as Fra Lippo Lippi is being arrested by the watch just before dawn. He speaks the poem to get himself out of the arrest, wisely giving his name and confessing that, although he is a monk, he has been visiting 'sportive ladies.' He also mentions that his patron is Cosimo di Medici and the captain of the watch becomes more respectful. Lippo's interest is caught by the torchlit faces of the men, and he wants to paint one of them as John the Baptist, even asking for chalk on the spot. The watch realise that he is 'the painter' and he appeals to their sympathy by telling how he has been locked up painting saints for weeks until this night's escapade. They are shocked that a monk should behave like this, but Lippo describes how he became a monk to save himself from starvation when he was just eight years old. His one talent turned out to be painting and he delighted in portraying real people. In his description of his first picture there is, however, a touch of real piety in the parenthesis about Christ, which reminds us that, sinner though he considers himself to be, he is also a monk. The Prior was upset by Lippo's realism and wanted him to paint 'men's souls'. But Lippo argues that physical beauty is a gift of God. He has to swallow his anger and paint 'saints' instead of real people. He complains that his critics have a hypocritical attitude to beauty, whereas he just praises God for it and doesn't try to transcend it. Again, liberal though his view is compared with the Prior's, we recognise the real piety in his idea of art. He foresees greater painters than himself will continue his work of realism, and believes that art is itself a gift of God to help mankind perceive the world. He is angry when people are offended by his realism. But here he quickly recovers his good temper in case he offends, and promises to paint a picture for the watch in which he will show himself lurking in a corner, befriended by a pretty girl-saint. After all, the serious old saints can't paint! Having talked the watch round, he scuttles off into the dawn just as he imagined himself scuttling into a corner in his projected picture.

NOTES AND GLOSSARY:
This is one of the liveliest and most serious poems in *Men and Women*. The cheerful, emphatic character of Lippo in no way detracts from the profundity of his idea of art and its function. His lapses into the real world are cleverly used by Browning to highlight the value of painting in understanding mankind, and his energetic enjoyment of the people around him is surely an indication that art cannot stray very far from reality without becoming false.

Browning wrote 'Fra Lippo Lippi' in Florence while he was studying Vasari's *Lives of the Most Eminent Painters* and Baldinucci's *Notes on the Painters*. The pictures Fra Lippo Lippi mentions are referred to in Vasari. Browning's use of his material is, however, highly imaginative: Lippo springs to life just as much as the purely imaginary characters which Browning created in *Men and Women*.

Lippo:	(l.1) Fra Lippo Lippi (*c*.1406–69), the Italian religious painter
Carmine:	(l.7) the convent of the Carmelite religious order
harry out:	(l.8) harrass
Cosimo di Medici:	(l.17) tyrant of Florence and patron of the arts (1389–1464)

John Baptist: (l.34) the saint who proclaimed Christ's coming; painted by Lippo at Prato

mew: (l.47) cage

Flower o' the broom . . .:   (ll.53–7) a snatch of a *stornello*, a Tuscan folk-song of improvised three-line stanzas

Saint Laurence: (l.67) the church of San Lorenzo

Jerome: (l.73) Lippo's picture of St Jerome is in the Uffizi in Florence

shucks: (l.84) pods or shells of vegetables

serge: (l.104) strong worsted woollen fabric

eight: (l.121) the eight magistrates of Florence

antiphonary: (l.130) music for the Psalms

Camaldolese: (l.139) another religious order

Preaching Friars: (l.140) the order of Dominicans

cribs: (l.148) pilferings, petty thefts

funked: (l.172) smoked (in this case, went out in smoke)

In that shape . . .:   (l.186) this refers to a medieval idea that the soul quits the body at death by flying out of the mouth. (See also note on 'puff of vapour' on page 24)

Giotto: (l.189) an Italian painter and architect (1267–1337)

Herodias: (l.196) the mother of Salome; implicated in the death of John the Baptist. See the Bible, Matthew 14

Angelico: (l.235) Fra Angelico (1387–1455), another monk-painter

Lorenzo: (l.236) Lorenzo Monaco (*c.*1370–1425), Fra Angelico's teacher

Guidi: (l.276) Tomaso Guidi Masaccio (1401–*c.*1428). Here Browning follows an error made by Vasari, as Masaccio was Lippo's teacher, not his pupil

Saint Laurence: (l.323) St Laurence was roasted alive for his beliefs

phiz: (l.327) face, physiognomy

wot: (l.337) knows

Sant' Ambrogio's: (l.346) Lippo painted *The Coronation of the Virgin* for this church

orris-root: (l.351) a fragrant root used for perfume

Saint John: (l.354) the patron saint of Florence

Saint Ambrose: (l.355) probably Ambrose the Camuldian (1386–1439), a friend of Cosimo di Medici

Iste perfecit opus: (l.372) (*Latin*) 'this man did the work'. This phrase is often placed in a painting to give the painter's name

kirtles: (l.380) skirts

Saint Lucy: (l.387) the patron saint of eyes, and so suitable to look after a painter. Lippo's picture portrays the Prior's mistress (or niece) in that role

7. A Toccata of Galuppi's

There is really only one speaker in this poem, but in stanzas 12–18 he imagines that the spirit of an eighteenth-century Venetian composer, Baldassaro Galuppi (1706–85), is addressing him. The speaker is a scientist who is listening to a showy, technical piece of music, or perhaps has just finished playing it himself. In spite of its gaiety and speed, the music saddens him. It conjures up Venice even though the speaker has never been out of England, and makes him imagine rich young Venetians pursuing their pleasures. He visualises a lady as if she were a portrait painting, just head and shoulders. These young people heard Galuppi's music but still ran after their empty pleasures. The music speaks to him, modern scientist though he be, with a cynical scepticism about the values of pleasure and science alike, telling him all such effort amounts to 'dust and ashes'.

NOTES AND GLOSSARY:
No one has yet found a toccata by Galuppi. It seems likely that Browning means the reader to imagine the music for himself, thus involving the reader imaginatively in the making of the poem. The sense of tawdry gaiety covering over melancholy knowledge of truth gives this poem its poignancy, but is well mediated through the character of the ageing scientist. There is an almost pagan quality in his idea of death as a place where you 'never see the sun'.

Toccata:	from (*Italian*) *toccare*, to touch; a rapid piece of keyboard music. Galuppi was a harpsichord player
Saint Mark's:	the cathedral of Venice. Wedding the sea with rings was a ritual symbolising Venetian supremacy of the seas
Shylock's bridge:	the Rialto
lesser thirds . . . sixths diminished . . . suspensions . . . solutions . . . sevenths . . . dominant . . . octave:	all musical terms used in harmony
tacitly:	silently. The Latin word *tacet* is used in music to indicate silence and is here used as a pun

8. By the Fire-side

This is one of Browning's most sympathetic love poems and has obvious links with his own marriage, but nevertheless the form is dramatic and it would be unimaginative to see the poem as a mere exercise in autobiography.

The speaker is looking forward to his old age, using the metaphor of the seasons to mellow the idea. He will sit poring over a book of Greek, but slip away into the world of memory, recalling happy youthful days in Italy. This opening is remarkable because in fact that happiness is the present, and the future 'memory' of it is only imaginary. The loving way he considers Italy prepares us for his discussion of his love for his wife. He will remember how they visited a ruined chapel, which he describes in minute detail, feeling the place to be 'silent and aware' as a prelude to the central mystery of the poem. He describes the perfect sympathy between himself and his wife as they sit by the fireside, and is confident that he will have the courage to recall how they found this harmony even when he grows old.

He tries to focus the exact moment at the ruined chapel when their ordinary 'obvious human bliss' was transformed into this perfect unity. The earlier description of the place is now brought to a fine sharpness as he pictures himself and his wife strolling there like lovers but still separate beings. They pause a moment on the bridge, and in that pause the 'screen' of separate self-hood is dissolved as his wife gives him her complete trust, which he had been afraid to demand from her. The very woods around them seem alive, and the speaker feels it was the magic of the forest which had 'mixed' them – before relapsing back into ordinary trees. It is only at such rare moments that an individual can be 'known', even to himself, and from them that his real acts will spring. This is why the speaker, watching his wife as she sits reading by the fireside, still feels the courage to return to that definitive moment.

NOTES AND GLOSSARY:

ruined chapel:	(l.31) the chapel is at Prato Fiorito and was visited by the Brownings in September 1853
Pella:	(l.43) a village in north-west Italy
November hours:	(ll.55–6) the 'hours' turn the leaf 'crimson' ('crimson' is used as a verb)
a shield . . . boss:	(l.58) the boss is the central stud in a shield
festa-day:	(l.77) a feast or saint's day
wattled cote:	(l.84) a rough hut made of sticks and mud
Five six nine:	(l.95) 1569, the date of the building
Leonor:	(l.101) Leonora is the 'perfect wife' in Ludwig van Beethoven's (1770–1827) opera, *Fidelio* (1805)
Great Word:	(l.132) see the Bible, Revelations 21:5
house not made with hands:	(l.135) see the Bible, 2 Corinthians 5:1
chrysolite:	(l.185) a precious stone

9. Any Wife to Any Husband

This poem deals with a subject which plainly intrigued Browning, the different kinds of expectation the two sexes have of love, and it provides a good contrast with poems such as 'A Woman's Last Word' or 'A

Serenade at the Villa'. Browning placed it after 'By the Fire-side as a significant contrast with the perfect moment of that poem. In 'Any Wife to Any Husband' the speaker is sure – and we have no reason to doubt – that she will die soon. This gives rise to her bitter reflections on her husband's love for her. She believes that he would go on loving her if she lived, because he is affectionate to her, and because the God-given quality of love itself would keep him true even when she grew to be old and ugly. (The reader, accustomed to Browning's oblique and subtle ways, may feel the speaker is protesting too much here.) But her tone alters at stanza 6 when her real opinion of her husband begins to emerge. She is bitter to think that, without her, he will 'sink' from the high ideal of their love. He is a sentimentalist, capable of treasuring a fleeting memory of her, but she wonders if he will be able to remain faithful to her when she's dead. She would like him to feel that she was his sun, other women just false fires, and to be prepared to wait for 'sunrise' to join his wife in heaven. But she expects he would argue that it would do no harm to her memory if he enjoyed the company of other women once she is dead. She concedes this bitterly, and tells him to go ahead and love 'new faces' – it cannot affect her ultimate claim on him. But she resents the fact that he will come to her dishonoured. Now if she were the one to survive, she would devote her life to his memory. There is something ironic in her feeling that, if he were dead, she could form his memory into her ideal man. Her only hope of his being faithful to her memory is if he sees it as a challenge. But her closing words show that she cannot believe he will rise to it.

NOTES AND GLOSSARY:

demesne:	estate, domain
plaudits:	praises, applause
bereft:	deprived
solace:	consolation
wilding:	growing in the wild
Titian's Venus:	probably Titian's (c.1490–1576) painting *Venus of Urbino* (1538) which is in the Uffizi in Florence
coronal:	garland or crown

10. An Epistle containing the Strange Medical Experience of Karshish

This poem takes the form of a letter, opening with Karshish's ceremonial address to his mentor, Abib, in which he expresses their mutual interest in the relation of body to soul, both in medicine and magic. He is writing from Bethany, outside Jerusalem, and will give the letter to a man whose eyes he has cured and who is too poor to repay him in any other way. The man may be untrustworthy, so Karshish decides to write about an interesting case but not to include medical secrets.

He begins to describe the case in purely medical terms, but it is the spiritual implications that really interest him. The patient, Lazarus, who believes he was raised from the dead, has so simple an outlook on life that it has astounded Karshish. Lazarus now lacks all sense of proportion in worldly things, as if he saw some invisible thread of the spiritual life in common events which makes him apathetic to common concerns. He is impatient only with 'ignorance and carelessness and sin', but restrains himself as a doctor would when faced with mere superstition. Unfortunately, the cure of Lazarus by a doctor from Nazareth took place years earlier and the doctor is now dead and cannot be questioned. He died about the time of the earthquake which signalled the death of Karshish's own master, but Lazarus believed him to be an incarnation of God. Mad though his idea is, Karshish is fascinated by the thought of God coming on earth to heal people like a doctor. He promises to write a more scientific letter from Jerusalem and closes this one with due ceremony. But even now, the possibility of a God with a 'human voice' and the compassionate heart of a physician attracts him. In true scientific spirit, he merely concludes, 'It is strange.'

NOTES AND GLOSSARY:

The speaker was invented by Browning but accurately placed in the historical context of the Roman Emperor Vespasian's invasion of Palestine (66AD). The case of Lazarus is from the Bible; see John 11:1–45.

Karshish:	(l.1) the name means one who gathers, a 'picker-up of learning's crumbs', as he says himself
puff of vapour:	(l.6) refers to the medieval idea that the 'wily vapour' (l.11) of the soul escapes from the body through the mouth when you die
term:	(l.12) appointed time
snakestone:	(l.17) ammonite
yellow balls:	(l.30) yellow eyeballs
scrip:	(l.40) small wallet or satchel
viscid choler:	(l.42) sticky bile
tertians:	(l.43) fevers which cause fits every other day
falling-sickness:	(l.44) epilepsy
wots:	(l.45) knows
runagate:	(l.49) vagabond
sublimate:	(l.50) purifying crystals
gum-tragacanth:	(l.55) gum used as a vehicle for drugs
porphyry:	(l.56) a hard stone used for a mortar
conceit:	(l.89) idea, notion
vantage:	(l.91) advantage
diurnal:	(l.102) everyday, daily

fume:	(l.103) hallucination, dream
Sanguine:	(l.109) of good colour, florid
laudable:	(l.110) sound, healthy
straitened:	(l.128) parsimonious, economical, close
witless:	(l.143) unknowing
pretermission:	(l.161) neglect
unadvisedly:	(l.170) rashly
Greek fire:	(l.177) combustible substance used by the Greeks for setting fire to enemy ships
proselytes:	(l.215) converts
affects:	(l.228) likes, has affection for
leech:	(l.247) doctor
borage:	(l.281) a medicinal herb
nitrous:	(l.282) containing potassium nitrate (saltpetre)
prolixly:	(l.285) wordily, at length

---

11. Mesmerism

The speaker in this poem wants to mesmerise the woman he loves to come to him, regardless of her own wishes. He tells his listener how he will do it. In the dead of night, he concentrates upon her image to 'have and hold' her form (Browning deliberately echoes the marriage service) in the room with him. Then he has to summon up her soul to complete the form. He 'commands' her soul to come to the empty form he has conjured up, moving his hands to mesmerise her. His fierce, possessive will is expressed in these gestures as a kind of fire which can irresistibly convince her soul. She feels suffocated and has to break out from the distant house where she is, as if it were from a coffin, and follow his command. She moves like a visionary through the stormy night towards him, driven by a sense of 'crowding peace' which he instils into her as she obeys him. This phrase is so extraordinary as to make the reader pause and doubt if she would wish to be so mesmerised. She enters the speaker's house, is heard on the stairs (in contrast with the eerie impersonal creaks of stanza 3), and with her hair flowing loose (in contrast with stanza 6) enters his room and miraculously combines with the mere physical form of herself that he originally conjured up. The passionately possessive love of the speaker is underscored by the strongly sexual connotations of the description he gives of her surrender to his will.

All this, however, is what he hopes will happen when he actually tries to mesmerise her. Before this, he will pray – as if he could bargain with God for the ownership of her soul, even though God will doubtless punish his impiety later. The final question is Browning's way of giving an ironic twist to the poem which lets the reader be certain that the poet does not consider the speaker to be so justified as he thinks himself to be. Compare this ending with that of 'Porphyria's Lover' in *Dramatic Romances* (1865).

NOTES AND GLOSSARY:
There was a fashion for mesmerism about 1844–5 which developed into a mania for spiritualism in the 1850s. Elizabeth Barrett firmly believed in it, but Browning was sceptical.

bar:	the bar of the fire grate which has a 'flag' of soot on it as it burns low
socket:	the last bit of the candle
calotypist:	calotype was the original form of photograph
behest:	bidding or command
tractile:	able to be drawn out

---

12. A Serenade at the Villa

There is something comical but also rather moving in the speaker's plight here. He is a rejected lover who none the less spent the previous night serenading his ex-mistress. It was a thickly warm, dark, stormy night when even the fireflies didn't shine, but he still 'wore' away the hours by singing to her. He hopes that she realised that, in spite of being rejected, he is still her faithful friend even until she becomes old and ugly – perhaps she will appreciate him then. But his more realistic fears tell him she is more likely to have hated his songs and his persistence, his undesired love and his gratuitous offer of 'help'. With poignant honesty, he recalls the fact that the villa remained dark against him while he sang, and her very lawn and garden gate seemed to detest him.

NOTES AND GLOSSARY:

fly:	firefly
worm:	glow-worm
forbore a term:	were quiet for a while
suspired:	sighed
hemlock:	an inauspicious flower here, being poisonous
Ground its teeth:	creaked as if in anger

---

13. My Star

This little poem is a simple expression of an idea which is found throughout Browning's work, which is that a person's particular view may be valid for him even if others don't see it. The speaker here has noticed a particular star which shines red and blue. His friends cannot see these colours, however – it is as if the star shines specially for him, and therefore he loves it.

NOTES AND GLOSSARY:
Browning used this as his autograph poem. In a letter to Elizabeth Barrett in November 1845, he called her his star and many critics have thought the poem to be about her.

spar:	crystalline mineral (for example, feldspar)
Saturn:	shines as a bright planet

14. Instans Tyrannus

The speaker here is the villain of the piece, and it is typical of Browning's oblique way of dealing with ideas that he should try to get inside the mind of this totally unsympathetic tyrant and see how it works. He loves power for its own sake, and he chose to victimise one man among his many subjects to whom he had taken an arbitrary dislike. The man was too low and insignificant for the tyrant to strike, so he tempted him with wealth – but the man resisted. Since he had neither friends nor relations, the tyrant could not hurt him in that way either. The very insignificance of the man safeguarded him, and so the tyrant felt powerless to hurt him. In frustration, he recognised that even a toad or rat can have a certain greatness if a great man is annoyed by it! He is determined to exterminate this man and finally manages to trap him. But as he sits back to enjoy the destruction, the poor man prays – and all the heavens and the earth leap to protect him and he is saved by God. At this display of superior power, the tyrant himself is afraid.

NOTES AND GLOSSARY:
The title comes from the first three lines of the Third Ode in Horace's *Odes* III:

Iustum et tenacem propositi virum
non civium ardor prava iubentium
non vultus instantis tyranni

(Neither the heat of the mob clamouring for wrong, nor the threatening visage of the angry tyrant, can shake the just man from his settled purpose.)

inveigle:	entice
perdue:	hidden
cates:	choice foods
spilth:	excess, overflow
pelf:	money, wealth
chafe:	irritation
nit:	the egg of a louse
gravamen:	grievance, the worst part of an accusation
marge:	margin

targe: shield
boss: centre stud of the shield

---

15. A Pretty Woman

Although you may prefer to consider that the speaker here is discussing a real woman, it is possible that Browning imagined him as looking at a charming picture of a pretty face, for he discusses the face almost like an object. Pretty though it is, the speaker feels that the face shows a superficial nature which might appeal to a man but would be incapable of returning love. Indeed, why demand any more of it than that it should be pretty? Why not appreciate that, and not expect more profound qualities? The speaker even suspects that a more profound nature would spoil the sheer prettiness of the face. He asks whether this prettiness deserves to be destroyed just because it may trap silly young men into love? To ask more than prettiness of such a face is to be like the man who would make a jewelled artificial rose to improve upon a real one: the jewel would just be hoarded by a greedy old king – the speaker prefers the natural rose. The best way to appreciate it is just to smell it and discard it when it fades!

NOTES AND GLOSSARY:
Browning's attitude to the speaker may be rather ironic – he makes him a young man who plainly likes pretty women, but does not intend to be caught by one himself. Browning's own unorthodox taste in feminine beauty is apparent in *Sordello* where he says: 'care-bit, erased, broken-up beauties ever took my taste supremely'.

brayed: pounded into small pieces
Scout: reject with disdain

---

16. 'Childe Roland to the Dark Tower Came'

The poem begins near the end of Roland's quest for the Dark Tower. By this time he is disillusioned with the quest and just longs for the end, so he takes the directions given him by the cripple even though he believes the cripple was lying. He feels like a man on his death-bed who overhears his friends making arrangements for his funeral, and can only feel a desire to die so as not to embarrass them: his friends have already failed in this quest, and he just wants to fail too. He turns from the road into a hideously mean landscape where nature itself seems to be waiting for the purgatorial fires of the Judgement Day to cleanse its diseased condition. The vegetation is battered as if by some huge brute, but the only creature visible is an aged, miserable blind horse, too degraded for even the devil to use any longer.

Roland shuts his eyes and tries to imagine happier days, but his memory only brings him the disgrace of his friends. He prefers the repulsive landscape of the present to such memories. He fords a river which is full of images of despair and death – the suicidal trees, the suspicion of corpses hidden under the water where he treads. But on the other side he finds no better country, only signs of violence and torture. He still seems as far from the Dark Tower as ever. An evil bird brushes past and makes him look up, and he sees, in the last light of evening, a ring of vicious mountains barring his way. But at that moment he seems to recognise the place – he has reached the Tower. The mountains crouch around him as if he were a hunted animal at bay. He hears the names of all the lost knights ringing in his ears, and sees their familiar forms as if wrapped in flames. None the less, undaunted, he puts the trumpet to his lips and sounds his challenge to the Dark Tower.

NOTES AND GLOSSARY:
Browning denied that this poem was intended to be an allegory, but said it came to him in a kind of dream which he felt impelled to write down.

Childe:	noble youth, aspirant to the knighthood
hoary:	grey- or white-haired
Askance:	sideways, suspiciously
descried:	caught sight of
estray:	stray creature or thing
cockle, spurge:	kinds of weeds
It nothing skills:	it is no use
Calcine:	refine or purge by burning
bents:	coarse grasses (or bent stalks in this context)
baulk:	hinder, prevent
Pashing:	crushing, breaking into pieces
colloped:	thick folds hanging (from his neck)
garniture:	adornment
howlet:	owl
bespate:	spattered, flecked
them:	themselves
no whit:	not at all
presage:	presentiment, expectation
pad:	tread down
plash:	muddy puddle
cirque:	arena
brake:	rack, instrument of torture
Tophet:	this used to mean Hell; see the Bible, Jeremiah 19:4–15
stubbed:	covered in stumps or stubs
rood:	about a quarter of an acre

Apollyon:	Satan
nonce:	time or present
heft:	hilt, handle
slug-horn:	used by Browning to mean trumpet. It is actually an old word for 'slogan' but Browning probably found it in Chatterton who also uses it to mean trumpet. Browning wrote an *Essay on Chatterton* in 1842; Chatterton (1752–70) was a poet who faked old manuscripts – the Rowley poems – and died in poverty.

---

17. Respectability

Here the speaker is talking to his lover about their lack of 'respectability', presumably because they are not married. If they were 'respectably' married, they would have wasted their lives before they discovered what a hypocritical sham 'respectability' really is. It pretends not to forbid love, but prescribes rules for it as an institution. Respectable marriage can be as hollow as the welcome Guizot gave to Montalembert at the Institut de France. The lovers would never have known what bliss the cold windy boulevards could offer, seeming warm and bright because they are so much in love with each other. He feels their way of love is better and encourages her to brave the night.

NOTES AND GLOSSARY:

Boulevart:	boulevard (in this case the streets in Paris)
Guizot and Montalembert:	the Institut de France required one of its members, François Guizot (1787–1874), to deliver the reception address for Charles Montalembert (1810–70) when he was elected a member of the Académie Française on 5 February 1852. Guizot was a constitutional royalist, whereas Montalembert was a liberal, and there was great personal enmity between the two men
lampions:	oil lamps with coloured glass

---

18. A Light Woman

This is a poem about love without being a love poem. The speaker is a cynic who thinks he has surprised a little bit of truth out of hiding. He asks his listener (who may be Browning himself) to judge which of the three people in his story, his friend, the light woman and himself, is most pitiable. The friend was being charmed by the flirtatious woman, so the speaker decided to save him from her wiles. He flirted with the woman himself to show his friend how faithless she was. He was older and more famous, and easily attracted her – too much so, in fact, for she gave herself to him 'indeed'. The speaker realises that his listener must find this rather disgusting, but begs him to hear out the tale. The friend now hates him; the woman loves him but will soon discover that he despises her – and even to himself he seems to be 'no hero'. He sees now that it is hard enough to save one's own soul, let alone play with another's. Yet he reminds his listener that he has proved he was right – the woman would have betrayed the friend. He has shown the 'truth' about her lightness. But, after all, what harm had she done him?

The final touch is most ingenious. The speaker makes a gift of the story to 'Robert Browning, you writer of plays' – but Browning has only given us the speaker's own words, not a 'play' about them. The speaker is, by implication, not a mouthpiece, but on the contrary the poet is serving the speaker! The poet, like the reader, doesn't know whom, in this triangle, to 'pity the most'. Further, it is implied that the poem is still in its state of raw material (that is, in the speaker's own words); or that the character of the speaker is actually the poetry, rather than his story. Thus the reader becomes involved not only with the moral question raised by the speaker, but also with the artistic question of the making of the poem.

NOTES AND GLOSSARY:
Browning wrote a number of plays up to 1846. He also wrote 'In a Balcony' (*Men and Women*) in 1853, and, since he always insisted that his poetry was 'dramatic in character', it is significant that he calls himself a 'writer of plays' here.

basilisk: a mythical reptile whose look or breath was fatal

---

19.   The Statue and the Bust

This poem tells the story of a bust and a statue in a square in Florence. The speaker is often thought to be voicing Browning's point of view, but this assumption is not necessary to an appreciation of the irony of the tale.

A bride on her wedding day saw a fine Duke riding by her window. He looked up and saw her and as their eyes met they fell in love. The Duke now had a purpose in life – to elope with the bride who had just married one of his courtiers. At the wedding banquet the husband noticed the looks which passed between his bride and the Duke and determined to keep his wife in the house henceforward. Her only contact with the outside world would be to watch, nun-like, at the window. She was determined to escape and elope with the Duke, and was only restrained by the thought of the pain this action would cause her aged father. She would wait. In the meantime, she could still watch the Duke pass her window each day. In just the same way, the Duke too put off the elopement because the husband was useful to him in State affairs. He too consoled himself by thinking he could see her as he rode by her window. Thus they procrastinated until the lady suddenly realised she was growing old, and had a portrait bust made to commemorate her beauty, which was to be placed in a niche by the window as if watching for the Duke. Bitterly she reflected that she had been no more active than a statue herself. At the same time the Duke too had a statue made of himself and put in the square. Bitterly he reflected that his soul seemed to have died before his body, and he imagined his ghost mocking such men as himself who cannot rouse themselves to action.

The teller of the story imagines that their two spirits cannot be in heaven. He expects the listener to object that the elopement would have been a crime, but he claims that even a crime can be as searching a test in the proving of souls as a good action. You can gamble with a forged coin as well as a true one – the thing that matters is to play for all you are worth. The lovers lost their game by inaction just as much as they might have lost it by acting. In the end, their crime was the sheer waste of their own potential. Perhaps many good people are guilty of such self-waste – this story is about you all!

NOTES AND GLOSSARY:

There are in fact two palaces mentioned in this poem: one from which the lady looks out, and where the bust is placed, and the other which is the Duke's palace in Via Larga where he holds the feast to celebrate the wedding of his courtier, the bridegroom. The Duke's palace is the one built by Cosimo di Medici in 1430. The one where the lady is imprisoned is probably the one now known as the Budini-Gattai Palace in Florence. The statue of the Duke, Ferdinand di Medici, stands in the square outside the Budini-Gattai Palace.

Great-Duke Ferdinand: (l.12) Ferdinand di Medici (1549–1608) who became Grand-Duke in 1587

Riccardi: (l.18) a noble family of Florence

coal-black tree: (l.21) tree from which ebony comes (*diospyros ebenos*)

encolure: (l.22) mane

emprise: (l.25) chivalrous enterprise

crime: (l.36) the overthrow of the Florentine Republic by Cosimo di Medici in 1434. This parenthesis shows the republican spirit of the speaker

catafalk: (l.57) open hearse

loop: (l.68) loophole

ave bell: (l.72) rung when 'Hail Mary' (Ave Maria) is to be said

Arno:	(1.94) main river in Florence
Petraja:	(1.95) a place north of Florence where the Duke owned a villa
simple:	(1.140) ignorant, foolish
Robbia:	(1.169) a family of sculptors in Florence
John of Douay:	(1.202) Giovanni di Bologna (1524–1608), the sculptor who carved the equestrian statue of Duke Ferdinand
pelf:	(1.232) wealth, money
Guelph:	(1.234) a coin, presumably called after the important faction of the same name
your table's a hat:	(1.238) using your hat to toss the dice, and for very small stakes
De te, fabula:	(1.250) (*Latin*) this story concerns you (Horace, *Satires* I)

---

20. Love in a Life and 21. Life in a Love

These two poems are a pair of variations on a theme, and are meant to reflect upon each other. In the first poem, the speaker uses the image of an immense house as an analogy for his life. He searches room after room for his mistress, but she always seems to go out just as he enters each room, so all he has left is traces of her presence. He feels his life is being used upon the search, but tries to keep up his hope of finding her in the end by making the most of his search, looking for his love in his life.

The second speaker is far more melancholy. He feels the nature of his relationship with his mistress is that she should always 'elude' his pursuit, even though he claims she can never finally 'escape' him. But he won't give up pursuing her as he feels that his whole life is contained in the pursuit of love. The last lines show that he realises that the very pursuit itself is somehow keeping him apart from her.

---

22. How it Strikes a Contemporary

The speaker is the 'contemporary' of an elderly poet in Valladolid in Spain. He describes the poet's appearance and habits, how he seemed to observe everything in an almost official way. Gossip had it that he was a spy or else the real governor of the town. The speaker wonders if the old man wrote reports for the King to read privately. He realises that this must sound absurd to his friend, but the appearance of the old poet was rather awe-inspiring and made one wonder whether he was involved in political intrigues. On the other hand, there was no evidence that he was in the King's pay, especially since the King changed his favourite so often. Perhaps the poet spied because he enjoyed the work, and the exercise of his superior perceptions was reward enough in itself, placing him above the ordinary folk as the King was above him. The speaker has checked one rumour and found it to be false – the old poet was not rich, but lived in an economical but respectable way. When he was a boy, the speaker had thought that a gaudily-dressed official was the town's governor, but had been corrected by his father who believed the old poet was the real 'Corregidor'. He wishes he could have been at the old poet's death-bed to see who would be there to take over his work from him, while he would be put aside just as he cast his old coat aside. Wryly the speaker comments on how well-dressed he and his friend are. Shrugging, he declares that he could never write poetry – strolling on the town's promenade is his idea of 'making the most of time.'

NOTES AND GLOSSARY:

The poet whose portrait is given here is deliberately made unromantic in his appearance and habits. Browning is offering an alternative to the more egotistical style of poet, such as Lord Byron. The essentially dutiful approach to life, the recording of reality as it is, like a report, the lack of personal aggrandisement, all these qualities are meant to contrast with the expected view of a poet. Browning's *Essay on Shelley* (1851) would suggest that this may be an 'objective' poet, a category in which he would have placed himself too.

Browning made an interesting change to the poem after 1855; in the first edition, all the pronouns referring to the King had capital letters (Lord, Me, His) but thereafter Browning changed them to lower case, as if to imply that the King was not to be confused with God. This change reflects Browning's care for keeping within the established context of a poem – just as the speakers in 'An Epistle of Karshish' and 'Cleon' are not actually converted to Christianity, so the speaker in this poem can see no further than the actual ruler of Spain for authority. The poet himself may serve a higher master. 'A poet's affair is with God,' Browning wrote to John Ruskin (in a letter of 10 December 1855), 'to whom he is accountable, and of whom is his reward.'

Valladolid:	a university town in Castile, the home of Cervantes
breathed themselves:	took their breath
ferrel:	metal tip
fly-leaf:	a broadsheet printed on one side
cognizance:	official observation
Too far above:	'[You are] Too far above my people – [and] beneath Me!'
Titians:	paintings by Titian (1488–1577)
Corregidor:	Spanish town governor or magistrate

23. The Last Ride Together

The lover in this poem has just been refused by his mistress. He takes this, but asks a last favour from her of one more ride together. Out of pity, she agrees and he feels like a god to be riding at her side once more and hopes the world will end that very night, almost hysterical with the momentary bliss of holding her as she climbs into the saddle. As they ride, the speaker feels no regret for his failure, realising that most men fail and few achieve even the bliss of a last ride. Ideals cannot be realised, but the heady pleasure of this last ride (as he watches his mistress's 'bosom heave' – plainly they are not proceeding at a sedate trot!) is worth far more than the futile sacrifices men make for 'glory'. Perhaps a poet could understand and describe his feelings, but he doubts whether a poet could *feel* them – to him, the ride is as wonderful as a poem. A sculptor could carve a Venus – but most men would prefer to see a real, live girl, and probably the sculptor would too! The composer of music devotes his life to a style which goes out of fashion, and the lover similarly has given his youth to this failed love, but he still has this last ride. In any case, even if he had married her, he would still have needed some impossible ideal to strive for, so to 'succeed' in winning her would have been a kind of failure too, whereas now she will remain his ideal. At this point he realises that she is being awfully quiet, but he hurries on, trying to persuade himself that this ride itself is a kind of achievement and desperately hoping it will last forever.

NOTES AND GLOSSARY:
As in 'A Lovers' Quarrel' and 'A Serenade at the Villa', Browning here makes the reader aware that this lover is not an embodiment of perfect love but a particular person with a personal passion. The reader is thus not really in a position to judge the events, but is given a vivid account of the speaker's feelings and thoughts.

demurs:	objects
deified:	made god-like
Abbey stones:	honour him by carving his name on the stones in Westminster Abbey
repine:	be discontented
sublimate:	idealise, exalt

24. The Patriot

The basis of this poem is the contrast between popularity and obloquy, all within the brief experience of the speaker himself. A year earlier he was the town's hero and saviour, who could ask for anything. Now he is entering the same town to be executed as a traitor. In both cases the public over-reacts to him, and he realises that both kinds of reception are dangerous. The adulation could make him proud and so cost him his place in heaven. The popular detestation at his execution is 'safer' for his soul, for now God owes him a reward for his unrecognised service to the people.

NOTES AND GLOSSARY:
In the first edition, Browning made the town in this poem Brescia in Lombardy, but in the edition of 1863 he removed the name of the town so that line 26 read: 'Thus I entered, and thus I go!' It is probable that he did this to ensure that readers did not think he meant any particular patriot to be the speaker. However, the poem may originally have referred to Arnold of Brescia, who was hanged in 1155. The poem in revised form clearly reflects the disappointment felt by both the Brownings at the speed with which the Florentines repudiated their new liberty and accepted back the Austrian Grand-Duke, Leopold II in April 1849.

Shambles: slaughter-house
requite: reward (altered to 'repay' in 1863)

---

25.   Master Hugues of Saxe-Gotha

In this monologue the organist in an old church ponders about the composer of the difficult music he has just performed, almost as if the ghost of Hugues is listening. He asks what the composer 'means' by his complicated fugues and goes on to answer his own question – needless to say the 'ghost' can't speak. He calls out to the sacristan to give him a few minutes longer before locking the church, which is now emptying after the evening service. He compares the echoing building with the organ as a 'house of sounds', and this parallel of sound and space is kept up throughout the poem. He also makes musical puns, as when the church saints go their 'rounds', or the 'rests' in the music when he looks out to see if Hugues's ghost is listening. The fugues are too difficult for young people – they are out of date, like the 'poor' organist himself – but he none the less feels they have something to say. He pictures Hugues as he appears in the engraving at the front of the book of fugues, with his face like part of a musical score (a kind of visual pun), listening and appraising his performance of the difficult Twelfth Fugue.

The candle is nearly burnt through by this time but the organist wants an answer, so he can prove the quality of this esoteric music to others. He examines the fugue itself as if it were a discussion, but cannot decide what it achieves. He compares the music's effect with the look of the church ceiling (he is up in the organ loft) which is elaborate but covered in cobwebs. He wonders if the overlay of obscurity, the 'cobwebs', may

not symbolise the way man busily covers up the true sky, blotting out
God's truth as the webs blot out the ornamental stars on the church
ceiling. Man's explanations obscure the truth, perhaps – but mankind
still feels that tradition should be respected, the webs should be left,
shouldn't they? He turns back to the fugue again, to try to see through
the 'cobwebs' of out-of-date musical fashion to Hugues's meaning. At
this moment the candle goes out, and the organist shouts to the sacristan
to give him some light, since he doesn't 'carry the moon' in his pocket.

NOTES AND GLOSSARY:

Saxe-Gotha:	a state in central Germany, now Thuringia, which contains Eisenach where Johann Sebastian Bach was born in 1685. Browning did not mean Hugues to be confused with Bach, but to be like one of the 'dry-as-dust' imitators of the composer. He invented Hugues (pronounced to rhyme with 'fugues')
colloquy:	conversation
sacristan:	the sexton, who looks after the church building, etc.
Aloys:	St Aloysius is the patron saint of youth; St Just was a child martyr. This concern with youth is an ironic touch, as the organist is concerned with old music which 'younger folk shelve'
helve:	handle
claviers:	keyboards
sciolists:	pseudo-scholars, pretenders to knowledge
shent:	stupefied, humiliated
parted the sheep from the goats:	see the Bible, Matthew 25:32. It originally refers to separating the virtuous from the wicked, but here probably means the real from the phoney
snuff:	burnt end
phrase:	musical theme on which the fugue is based
propound:	a pun on *proposta*, the musical subject
discept:	contend
bandied:	tossed about
vociferance:	shouting
crepitant:	crackling sound
strepitant:	noisy (a pun on musical term *strepito*)
O Danaides, O Sieve!:	the Danaides in Greek legend, as punishment for murdering their husbands, were condemned for ever to try to fill a sieve with water
casuist Escobar:	Antonio Escobar y Mendoza (1589–1667), a Jesuit theologian whose theory of 'probabilism' was to justify the means by the ends. A casuist is a person whose arguments are more subtle than sound

Est fuga, volvitur rota!: (*Latin*) it has flown, the wheel turns!

risposting: replying (a pun on musical term *risposta* which refers to the answering voice in a fugue)

groining: the intersection of the vaults in the church roof

tickens: ticking, very coarse cloth for coverings

Palled: cloaked in funeral cloth

usurpature: encroachment

glozes: glosses, explanations

make up a visage: pull a face

mountain in labour: a reference to Horace, *Ars Poetica*: 'A mountain went into labour and brought forth a little mouse' – that is great efforts bringing little results

mea poena: (*Latin*) for my pains

Gorgon: a mythical creature in Greek legend whose look turned men to stone

mode Palestrina: Palestrina (1525–94) began bringing counterpoint into music. Browning wrote that it was 'the name given ... to a certain simple and severe style like that of the master [Palestrina]'

---

26. Bishop Blougram's Apology

The Bishop has been entertaining a young journalist, Gigadibs, to dinner, and after the meal he answers the young man's criticisms. Thus the monologue takes the rhetorical form of a defence, much of which is an attack on the half-baked idealism of Gigadibs himself.

The Bishop opens by frankly and confidentially admitting to certain commercial aspects of the church, leading up to 'So you despise me, Mr Gigadibs.' He doesn't mean Gigadibs 'despises' him in a worldly sense – no doubt the journalist will later boast of having had dinner with a Bishop – but he despises the Bishop for his lack of ideals, his insincerity. Gigadibs probably thinks the Bishop is sceptical and not a true believer, like an actor who is playing the role of Death but finds himself confronted with death itself after the play. Thus though the Bishop has achieved so much of his ambition and Gigadibs so little, Gigadibs still thinks himself his superior in ideals. But the Bishop does not agree. Life is practical, not ideal, and the problem is how to make the best of what exists. He compares life to a voyage where the cabin is one's living space. Gigadibs would bring his idealist clutter, and finding there was no room for it would bring nothing on his voyage. But the Bishop would be ingenious, everything he brought would be specially designed for a cabin and would give him a comfortable voyage. Now, he asks Gigadibs, why don't you also make a comfortable trip – 'be a Bishop too'? What are his criticisms of the Bishop's luggage?

First, the problem of faith: no one sensible could believe all the Christian dogma the Bishop professes. The Bishop doesn't discuss this here, but agrees to give it up if Gigadibs agrees to give up his idealism for the purposes of argument. But how can they remain unbelievers – won't they have bouts of faith, as they now have fits of doubt? Christian faith may look like a plain broad track from a distance, but when you are on it it is intermittent, just as Gigadibs's scepticism is punctuated by belief. So disbelief is no better than belief. In fact, the Bishop claims, it is worse. Returning to his shipboard analogy, he shows how faith gives him a more comfortable journey through life than unbelief could. To achieve this he must declare he has absolute faith, of course; he compares his moments of doubt with mere troublesome dreams, such as no sane man would consider more important than his waking, rational existence – faith. Gigadib's scepticism shows him to be a dreamer – he should stay in bed! Would that win him the world's respect? He points out that his faith has made him a Bishop. This is a clever twist because it changes the issue from being one of honest feeling to one of worldly wisdom, where the Bishop is plainly superior. He is playing with Gigadibs, calling him 'friend' and making a display of frankness.

The Bishop now argues a different point: some decisions in life are once and for all – marriage and religion, for example. Blougram was born a Christian and likes the forms of his Church which give him the respect and power he desires. A life of unbelief has no forms which could give these things. If Gigadibs thinks this displays a meanly opportunist character, the Bishop's reply is that he did not make his own nature. Here too he has had to do the best with what was given, just as he would with cramped cabin-space. This pragmatism may have won him popular recognition, but Gigadibs considers it degrades him in the eyes of noble and clever men. Not at all, counters the Bishop, as no one is ever sure whether he is a charlatan or not – he keeps even the cleverest guessing. Gigadibs's own ideals are so obvious that they are a bore, but the Bishop is a man of his times and walks a tightrope between faith and doubt, watched by all. Besides, if Gigadibs is right and there is no afterlife, the Bishop will still have had a better life by professing faith than Gigadibs professing doubt. Even Gigadibs's own hero, Shakespeare, would certainly have preferred to be a rich bishop himself than just imagine one as a character in a play. Men of real genius, notes the Bishop, do not share Gigadibs's attitude! Once the usefulness of faith is admitted, the whole argument alters. He himself admires Luther's faith, but he cannot achieve it himself. None the less even his own imperfect faith has real value – the argument is 'back on Christian ground'. No matter if he doubts, so long as his whole life advances God's purpose of defeating evil. If Gigadibs admits Christianity is attractive, then that is enough faith to begin with. Pure faith is virtually impossible. God works through doubts as well as faith, even through evil. The Bishop welcomes doubt – like a pinch of snuff – to excite his sense of faith. He protests that this modern kind of belief is as good as the medieval faith which never openly doubted but did not stop men from committing crimes. He sees the struggle between good and evil as the means of awaking the soul. No faith can be as strong as the belief that fire can give you a burn. But so long as doubts are overcome by faith, faith is enough. This is why the Bishop refuses to express scepticism about miracles – his doubts make him value even the doubtful parts of his religion. And this allows him to pursue his ambitions within the Church and to appreciate the gift of life to the full. To neglect the present would be to miss God's purpose. It is appropriate to be 'worldly in this world', by Gigadibs's own admission. If the rationalistic view of life is right, why does Gigadibs pretend to be morally superior? He is as much a conventional sheep as the rest of the Bishop's flock. But Blougram himself is not content to be just another sheep. If they both died that very night, the Bishop would be satisfied with his life, whereas the biggest thing in Gigadibs's would be dinner with the Bishop!

Giving him notice of dismissal by offering him a 'last' glass of wine, the Bishop urbanely pours contempt on Gigadibs. He doesn't even bother to ask him to keep their conversation secret. No one would believe Gigadibs. If he were in any way remarkable, the Bishop would accept his right to criticise, but he is just a second-rate journalist. Patronisingly, the Bishop gives him a card with a tiny scrawl of pencil on it to help him to get work on magazines in Dublin or New York. He is certain Gigadibs no longer 'despises' him.

The closing sections of the poem are impersonally narrated and confirm our impression that the Bishop was not being sincere with Gigadibs. But the effect on the young man is unexpected – instead of building his journalistic career on this evening with the Bishop, he emigrated to lead the simple life and study the Bible for himself!

NOTES AND GLOSSARY:

Pugin:	(l.6) the Gothic Revival architect (1812–52), who was converted to Roman Catholicism in 1836. He built St Chad's Cathedral in Birmingham 1839–42
entourage:	(l.26) attendants, household
Corpus Christi:	(l.34) the Thursday after Trinity Sunday, the feast of the Body of Christ (Eucharist)
Che che:	(l.45) (Italian) an exclamation, roughly equal to 'Come, come'
Goethe:	(l.52) Johann Wolfgang von Goethe (1750–1832), German poet, playwright and philosopher
Buonaparte:	(l.53) Napoleon Buonaparte (1769–1821), Emperor of France

D'Orsay:	(l.54) Count Blessington D'Orsay (1801–52), a famous dandy. (See also Introduction, page 11)
tire-room:	(l.70) dressing room
shift himself:	(l.71) change his clothes
Balzac:	(l.108) Honoré de Balzac (1799–1850), the prolific French novelist
Leipsic:	(l.111) the Teubner series of books began to appear in 1849
Parma's pride:	(l.113) a picture of St Jerome by the Italian painter Correggio (1489–1534)
marvellous Modenese:	(l.117) Correggio studied painting at Modena
The Way:	(l.197) Christ said, 'I am the Way.' See the Bible, John 14:6
Comport:	(l.283) suit, be fitted to
street's stones:	(l.315) 'If thou be the Son of God, command that these stones be made bread.' (the Bible, Matthew, 4:3)
Peter:	(l.316) St Peter was the first Pope
Hildebrand:	(l.316) Pope Gregory VII (1073–85), whose creed emphasised the power of the Church's hierarchy
winking Virgin:	(l.377) Cardinal Newman defended the idea that the Virgin's eye in some paintings might miraculously wink
Verdi:	(l.381) Giuseppe Verdi (1813–1901), the Italian opera composer. His opera *Macbeth* was performed in Florence in 1847
Rossini:	(l.386) Gioacchino Rossini (1792–1868), another opera composer
demireps:	(l.397) ladies of doubtful reputation
Schelling's way:	(l.411) Friedrich Schelling (1775–1854), a German philosopher who wrote on *Transcendental Idealism*
Peter's chains:	(l.425) Peter's chains were miraculously removed. See the Bible, Acts 12:7
'The State, that's I':	(l.466) a saying attributed to Louis XIV of France, possibly quoted by Napoleon
Austrian marriage:	(l.472) in 1810 Napoleon married Marie-Louise of Austria
Austerlitz:	(l.474) Napoleon beat Russia and Austria at Austerlitz in 1805
Guilio Romano:	(l.516) an Italian painter (1492–1546)
Dowland:	(l.516) John Dowland (1563–1626), an English composer and lutenist
Pandulph:	(l.519) a character in Shakespeare's (1564–1616) play, *King John*

views:	(l.533) pictures on the Bishop's wall
shut book:	(l.572) Luther had the Bible translated
Strauss:	(l.577) David Friedrich Strauss (1808–74), a German theologian who wrote *The Life of Jesus* (1835), denying the miracles
'What think ye ....:	(l.626) the Bible, Matthew 12:42
ichors:	(l.664) ichor is a watery discharge from a wound which helps healing
Michael's foot:	(l.667) the Archangel Michael subdued Satan, who is often portrayed in the form of a serpent under his foot
box:	(l.669) snuff box
cosmogony:	(l.679) theory of the creation of the universe
Ararat:	(l.685) Mount Ararat is where Noah's Ark landed (see the Bible, Genesis 8:4)
Brother Newman:	(l.703) John Henry Newman (1801–90) was converted to Roman Catholicism in 1845 and believed in miracles; he later became Cardinal Newman
Immaculate Conception:	(l.704) the Immaculate Conception was declared Roman Catholic doctrine by Pope Pius IX in 1854
Bomba's Lazzaroni:	(l.715) King Bomba was the nickname of Ferdinand II of Sicily; Lazzaroni are beggars
Antonelli:	(l.716) Cardinal Antonelli, secretary to Pope Pius IX
Naples' Liquefaction:	(l.728) a miracle defended by Newman in 1851
decrassify:	(l.732) refine, remove grossly stupid parts
excrescence:	(l.740) abnormal growth
Fichte:	(l.744) Johann Gottlieb Fichte (1762–1814), a German philosopher who wrote *Critique of Revelation*, claiming that man invented God
purblind:	(l.756) dull, half-blind
Scouts:	(l.791) derides, treats with scorn
natural religion:	(l.819) religion based on natural phenomena as opposed to revelation or miracles
a Pan's face:	(l.868) Pan was the Greek god of shepherds, half goat, half man. (The 1855 edition read 'man's face')
Pastor est ...:	(l.877) 'the Lord is your shepherd'. See the Bible, Psalm 23
maw:	(l.880) stomach
fictile:	(l.914) earthenware, made of clay
Albano:	(l.915) Roman ruins south-east of Rome
Anacreon's Greek:	(l.915) Anacreon was a Greek lyric poet of the sixth century BC

self-abnegating:	(l.933) self-denying
this war:	(l.938) the Crimean War began in March 1854
drugget:	(l.942) coarse cloth
Blackwood's Magazine:	(l.945) a well-thought-of periodical
Whitechapel:	(l.951) a slum district of East London
in Dublin:	(l.957) Cardinal Wiseman founded *The Dublin Review* in 1836
in partibus . . .:	(l.972) (*Latin*) the Bishop's Latin title – 'Bishop in regions, and also' – was changed in 1850
nomenclature:	(l.995) terminology
cavillers:	(l.998) quibblers
Oppugn:	(l.999) attack
St John:	(l.1013) this book of the Bible contains the Miracle of the Fishes

---

27. Memorabilia

The speaker, an ardent admirer of Shelley, has met a man who actually knew Shelley. The incident is compared by the speaker to his finding an eagle's feather on a dreary moor, but the man who actually met Shelley thinks the speaker's reaction is comical.

NOTES AND GLOSSARY:

Memorabilia:	(*Latin*) memorable things

---

28. Andrea del Sarto

The painter is in a peaceful mood as he sits at evening with his beautiful wife, Lucrezia, but it is plain from his opening words that this harmony is unusual for them. If she will just sit a while with him, he will paint better tomorrow and earn the money she wants. He takes her hand, admires her, evidently thinking how he will paint her and save money by not employing a model. In his pictures, her beauty becomes available to everybody, though she never seems to give herself to any. The light fades as they sit, and seems to underline the greyness of Andrea's mood. Passively he supposes God has ordered it all. His wife doesn't understand his painting, but he tells her how his work is praised. In himself he knows it lacks the vital spark which often animates the works of less skilful masters. For instance, he has a copy of a picture by Raphael, where Raphael has drawn an arm incorrectly: he, Andrea, could draw it correctly, but would miss the 'soul' which animates Raphael's picture.

He blames his wife for not inspiring him – her beauty alone, without a mind to go with it has proved insufficient. She may even have held him back – the other great artists, Raphael and Michelangelo, had no wives.

Still maybe God will compensate Andrea for the lack of success on earth. Here he is insulted by the French lords in Florence because he stole money from his patron, King Francis of France, and used it to build the house for his wife. He remembers the fruitful period of that patronage before he married Lucrezia. Still, as he looks at her, he feels that men may say that though Raphael was the greater painter, Andrea's 'virgin was his wife.' This remarkable phrase, suggestive of total frustration of Andrea's marriage, is used with ambivalence by Browning even though it is clearly meant by Andrea to refer to Lucrezia's being his model. Andrea still regards the Raphael and, recalling how Michelangelo praised him, he chalks in a correct arm in a sudden flush of confidence – only to rub it out the next moment in despair. This momentary confidence and rapid backsliding into lethargy are typical of Andrea's character, as witness his brief glory with Francis, or his passive acceptance of his wife's infidelity after the violence of his first passion for her. He plainly bores her by his talk, but tries to flatter her and is delighted when she smiles (in fact, she has heard her lover arriving). But even as Andrea whiningly pleads with her to smile and love him, she moves away and he resigns her without much regret. Idly, he hopes he may be recognised as being as great as Raphael, Michelangelo and Leonardo in heaven – where he will still be beaten by them because Lucrezia will still drag him down. He sends her off to meet her lover.

NOTES AND GLOSSARY:

Andrea del Sarto: (title) del Sarto (1486–1531), 'the faultless painter' in Vasari's *Lives of the Most Eminent Painters*. He was in France 1518–19, and the poem is set in 1525

Fiesole: (1.15) a village outside Florence

Someone says: (1.76) 'someone' turns out to be Michelangelo (1.199)

Morello: (1.93) a mountain near Florence

The Urbinate: (1.105) Raphael (1483–1520), the Italian painter

George Vasari: (1.106) Giorgio Vasari (1512–74), painter and art historian

Agnolo: (1.130) Michelangelo (1475–1564), painter and sculptor

Francis: (1.149) King Francis I of France

Fontainebleau: (1.150) a small town near Paris where Francis I built a famous palace

frank: (1.160) punning on 'French'

The Roman: (1.178) Raphael worked in Rome

cue-owls: (1.210) scops owls, whose call is 'kiu' (cue)

meted: (1.262) measured

angel's reed: (1.262) angel's measuring rod. See the Bible, Revelations 21:15

Leonard: (l.263) Leonardo da Vinci (1452–1519), painter and inventor

---

29. Before and 30. After

This pair of poems takes place 'Before' and 'After' a duel. The first speaker is one of the seconds, discussing the forthcoming duel and the principle of duelling with the other second. The 'guiltless' party (he doesn't say 'innocent') will be rewarded by God, who alone can judge the argument. Surely men should be allowed to defend their honour. One duellist must be insincere in his defence, and carry the knowledge of his sin. He must feel as if heaven and earth know his secret, even though they don't disclose it. His guilt will dog his tracks till he longs for the release, even into punishment. The guiltless man, on the other hand, is sure to be rewarded for his honourable act by God even if he is killed, and his courage will set the seal on his faith in his own righteousness. The speaker responds savagely to the suggestion that the guiltless man could 'forgive' the other. The speaker is adamant that the only forgiveness will be if the guilty man is killed. Anyway, the guilty man still has time to confess – if he won't, let the duel go ahead. The speaker is conspicuously in favour of the fight to end the quarrel, and the fact that his own skin is in no danger must make us a little suspicious about his motives.

The second poem presents the human, not the rhetorical, case: now the victorious duellist speaks, without any of the high-falutin moral bombast of the first speaker. This speaker just records the horror of having killed a man, looking at the corpse's face. The reasons for the duel have become irrelevant. The speaker can only wish hopelessly that they could be boys together once more – how easy it would be to forgive the 'wrong' then! But all that remains are the facts of the one living and the one dead man.

NOTES AND GLOSSARY:
'Before'

entoilment:	being trapped in the toils/snares
caps to:	takes his hat off to
misfeasance:	transgression (in a legal sense). Here the word is used rather jocularly

---

31. In Three Days and 32. In a Year

The lover will see his mistress in 'three days and just one night' – but the days of summer seem too long, though the nights are short. He plunges back into a sensual memory of her when she let him caress her hair, comparing its colour to the gold tints of 'early Art'. But her absence also gives rise to fears: the world might suddenly change in these three days!

If it doesn't, he should be thankful. Another, he says a lesser, fear is that his life with his mistress may bring difficulties and disappointments. But he shakes this off, returning to the safe limits of his expectations – 'in three days'.

In contrast to this, the woman who speaks 'In a Year' is at the end of her love affair. She doesn't know what went wrong, but remembers how her lover thought everything she did was wonderful at the start of their love. When he declared he loved her, she admitted that she already loved him too – why should he be the only one to give in the relationship? But perhaps she made it too obvious. If he still loved her, she would find other ways of giving herself to him, so that he would only realise how much she loved him when she died for him. It would be pure flattery for him. But the repulsive implications of this picture of self-sacrifice strike her in the last stanza. In a detached way, she awaits his breaking-off of the affair. The very earth under her feet might once have been the heart of a man, she reflects – the idea triggered off by her romantically empty fancy of dying for him. The 'cold clod' is more authentic and more instructive, for her mind now turns to larger questions – 'what comes next? Is it God?' – which put the broken affair into perspective.

NOTES AND GLOSSARY:
The contrast between these two poems is tinged with the unselfconscious humour which marks most of Browning's poems above love. Either poem by itself might be taken too seriously by a romantically inclined reader, but the two in juxtaposition provide a commentary so dry and yet so sympathetic that the emotions described seem to belong entirely to the speakers. They do not put forward abstract truths nor preach at the reader, because their concerns are intrinsic to their situations.

---

33. Old Pictures in Florence

The speaker here is a lover of early Italian painting who is telling his hearer of his thoughts as he looked over Florence on a warm March morning. The sight of Giotto's bell-tower impressed him especially strongly on this morning (we find out why in stanza 30) and he broods on his life's work of researching forgotten painters and their works. He feels the ghosts of these neglected artists still haunt Florence where their works are crumbling away. More famous painters, such as Michelangelo and Raphael, must have left the earth by now, he feels, but the 'wronged great souls' of earlier masters still seek justice and recognition. This is why he is addressing the listener whose ignorance is what prevents him from appreciating them. He sketches a history of art, from the Greek ideals of superhuman beauty of physique, to the more spiritual values which are sought in the early Italian masters he loves. Giotto's great bell-tower is still incomplete: his work of 'perfection' was just the drawing of a circle. Once man began to search for spiritual rather than visible truth in art, imperfection itself became valid since perfection was held to be achieved only in the next life. This is why he loves the early masters such as Pisano, Cimabue, Ghiberti and Ghirlandaio, and works for their recognition and the preservation of their frescoes. But he has a grievance against their ghosts: why don't they reveal their lost works to him? He wouldn't expect to find a famous painter's work, but why not one by a minor master? How ungrateful the ghosts are, letting their paintings fall into the hands of some rich but tasteless purchaser! He is particularly hurt that a picture by Giotto was recently discovered by someone else. He can only hope to possess it some day. In the meantime he optimistically prophesies the return of Florentine freedom so that painting can be reborn, and a Tuscan-speaking citizen will propose the completion of Giotto's bell-tower, perfecting the city and symbolising Italian freedom.

NOTES AND GLOSSARY:
The main sources for this poem are Browning's own interest in art and his study of Vasari.

aloed:	(l.3) covered in aloes (succulent plants)
bell-tower:	(l.15) Giotto (1267–1337), the painter and architect, designed the Campanile (bell-tower) in Florence. It was begun in 1334 but has never been completed
chaffer:	(l.33) bargain, haggle over the price
apsis:	(l.38) apse, the rounded end of a church
Michaels and Raphaels:	(l.51) Michelangelos and Raphaels and painters of their period
Dellos:	(l.64) painters such as Dello di Niccolo (Niccolo Fiorentino, 1403–71)
girns:	(l.67) snarls
Stefano:	(l.69) Stefano Fiorentino (1301–50) was a pupil of Giotto's
dole:	(l.81) charity, gift
in fructu:	(l.84) as fruit
Theseus:	(l.98) a Greek hero, king of Athens
Son of Priam:	(l.99) Priam was king of Troy and his sons included Hector and Paris
Apollo:	(l.101) the Greek god of the Muses, who killed the Python at Delphi
Niobe:	(l.102) in Greek legend a queen who wept for the deaths of her children until she turned to a stone
racers' frieze:	(l.103) a procession of horsemen on the Parthenon
dying Alexander:	(l.104) Alexander the Great died when he was only thirty-two

'O!':	(l.135) a perfect circle drawn by Giotto when an envoy from the Pope asked him for a picture on the spot. The tale comes from Vasari's *Lives*
fray:	(l.149) rub away
quiddit:	(l.156) quibble (quiddity)
allocution:	(l.159) lecture, formal speech
congeries:	(l.165) masses
Nicolo the Pisan:	(l.179) Nicolo Pisano (c.1225–c.1284), a sculptor and architect
My painter:	(l.180) Giovanni Cimabue (1240–1302), a painter who taught Giotto
Ghiberti:	(l.182) Lorenzo Ghiberti (1381–1455), a sculptor
Ghirlandajo:	(l.182) Domenico Curradi Ghirlandaio (1449–94), also called Bigordi in l.201, taught Michelangelo. Browning owned a picture attributed to him
critic-meed:	(l.183) critical reward, favourable opinion
dree:	(l.198) suffer, endure
out-ferreted:	(l.199) searched out
Bigordi:	(l.201) Ghirlandaio (see above)
Sandro:	(l.202) Sandro Botticelli (1444–1510), Florentine painter
wronged Lippino:	(l.203) Lippino (1457–1504), a painter, was the illegitimate son of Fra Lippo Lippi
Fra Angelico:	(l.204) Florentine painter (1387–1455)
Taddeo Gaddi:	(l.205) Gaddi (c.1300–66) was a pupil of Giotto's
intonaco:	(l.206) plaster used as background of a fresco
Lorenzo Monaco:	(l.208) Monaco (1370–1425) was a Florentine painter
Pollajolo:	(l.210) Antonio Pollaiuolo (1432–98), a painter and goldsmith. Browning owned a picture attributed to him
tempera:	(l.214) distemper (fresco technique)
Alesso Baldovinetti:	(l.215) Baldovinetti (1427–99) was a Florentine painter
Margheritone of Arezzo:	(l.217) a Sienese painter (c.1230–c.1300)
barret:	(l.218) a biretta, the flat cap worn by a priest
Zeno:	(l.230) Zeno of Citium, the founder of Stoicism
Carlino:	(l.232) Carlo Dolci (1616–86), a pious painter
little tablet:	(l.237) Vasari claimed that Michelangelo owned a small picture by Giotto of the Death of the Virgin, but that the picture was lost
San Spirito ... Ognissanti:	(ll.241–2) the speaker is unsure which church contained the picture by Giotto, but Vasari says it was Ognissanti (All Saints)

Detur amanti:	(l.244) (*Latin*) 'it is to be given to him who loves it'
Koh-i-noor:	(l.245) the famous diamond given to Queen Victoria in 1849
Giamschid:	(l.246) a legendary king of Persia who had a remarkable ruby
dotard:	(l.249) a foolish old man, in this case Count Radetzky (1766–1858) who was Austrian governor of Northern Italy
Saint Gothard:	(l.251) a pass in the Alps
Radetzky:	(l.255) see above
Morello:	(l.256) a mountain outside Florence
stone of Dante:	(l.258) a paving stone where Dante was said to have sat, mentioned in *Casa Guidi Windows* by Elizabeth Barrett Browning (see below)
witanagemot:	(l.259) the Anglo-Saxon parliament
Casa Guidi:	(l.260) *Casa Guidi Windows* was the title of a poem (1851) by Elizabeth Barrett Browning on Italian freedom, taken from the name of the house where the Brownings lived in Florence
quod videas ante:	(l.260) (*Latin*) 'which you may have seen before'
Lorraine:	(l.263) the Austrian tyrants belonged to the house of Hapsburg-Lorraine
Orgagna:	(l.264) Orcagna (Andrea di Cione), a Florentine painter, active 1344–68
fructuous:	(l.269) fruitful
Chimaera:	(l.271) a Greek mythical monster with a lion's head, goat's body and dragon's tail
'*issimo*':	(l.274) the superlative ending in Italian
Cambuscan:	(l.275) the unfinished tale of the Squire in Geoffrey Chaucer's (*c.*1340–1400) *Canterbury Tales*
alt to *altissimo*:	(l.276) high to highest
beccaccia:	(l.277) (*Italian*) woodcock
Duomo:	(l.278) cathedral
braccia:	(l.279) Italian measure, cubit (about 2 ft). Giotto's bell-tower was meant to have a 50-ft spire (never built)
'God and the people':	(l.285) Mazzini's motto. Mazzini was an Italian statesman involved in the Unification of Italy
tricolour:	(l.286) the Italian flag

34. In a Balcony

There are only three characters in this closet-drama: Norbert, the young prime minister who has just succeeded in a diplomatic coup; Constance, the Queen's cousin whom Norbert loves; and the Queen herself, who is now middle-aged and was technically betrothed as a baby though the marriage never took place. Norbert and Constance are arguing over how to gain the Queen's consent to their marriage. He is for asking directly, but she expects that the Queen would dismiss him for such a request as she would realise that he had been serving her in order to win Constance. She wants him to tell the Queen that, since he can never aspire to love her, he has decided to ask for Constance, her maid, as the next best thing. Norbert is unhappy at the subterfuge, but is persuaded by Constance's insistence that she understands the Queen better than he does, and he dashes off to ask the Queen.

The Queen now enters the Balcony to see Constance, breathlessly demanding, 'Is it true?' Constance, thinking Norbert has made their request, assures her that 'it' is true, but the Queen is talking about being too old for love and yet feeling love to be the only good thing in life. Constance begins to suspect her plan has miscarried, and discovers that the Queen has taken Norbert's flattery literally. The Queen admits that she had thought Norbert was in love with Constance and was expecting them to marry – but now she has discovered that Norbert really loves her, not Constance. She uses the very words Constance told Norbert to say to prove it. Rather weakly, Constance reminds her of her childhood betrothal, but the Queen is determined to brush all objections aside.

The last part opens with Constance protesting her undying love to Norbert. He is unsuspicious enough to be pleased by this, not having realised the effect that he has had on the Queen. He is kissing Constance as the Queen enters the Balcony. Instantly, Constance begins to make excuses and tries to hand her lover over to the Queen for his own good – but Norbert refuses to be handed over. The Queen now passionately declares her love for him, but Norbert assumes that this a formal, not a personal, declaration, and asks for permission to marry Constance. Constance tries to interpose and make him marry the Queen, but he finally loses patience with her and tells her how insulting to his love her behaviour is. He angrily re-affirms that he can only love one woman, and that woman is Constance herself. Is Constance trying to test him by these tricks? By this time the Queen realises what is going on, and she exits silently. Constance, who is woman enough to be secretly pleased by this dramatic exhibition of Norbert's love, flings herself into his arms and avoids explanations. A guard is heard approaching the Balcony as they embrace.

NOTES AND GLOSSARY:
Browning wrote seven plays between 1837 and 1846, and 'In a Balcony' was written in 1853. At first, he divided the piece into three parts but in 1863 he made the action continuous and called it 'In a Balcony – a Scene'.

Hold you and have you: (l.17) a deliberate echo of the marriage service

cognizant: (l.27) aware

Pictures all round her!: (l.107) an imaginary gallery of pictures, but it has much in common with Dulwich Gallery which Browning knew well

Rubens: (l.130) Peter Paul Rubens (1577–1640), Flemish painter

sleights: (l.191) tricks

telegraphs: (l.192) signals or signs

to pant and reach: (l.246) to strive for and attain

paedagogic: (l.284) teacherish, didactic

Dissertate: (l.324) give a discourse

conceit: (l.333) idea

Mother: (l.342) Christ's mother, the Virgin Mary

baladine: (l.412) a woman who dances in public, street-dancer

halbert: (l.422) halberd, a combination of spear and battle-axe

in intelligence: (l.445) aware of it

paragon: (l.497) model of excellence

Triton: (l.516) Greek sea-god with fish tail

Nymph: (l.516) a minor goddess in Greek mythology

phantasy: (l.529) (fantasy) imagination

largess: (l.613) gifts freely given

educe: (l.652) develop, draw out

tithe: (l.686) tax (one tenth)

plastic: (l.703) able to mould or shape (them)

and you by: (l.703) if you are by

The Graces: (l.712) usually three Greek goddesses

stalking-horse: (l.742) pretext

constant: (l.765) here punning on 'Constance'

overcharge: (l.795) overact, overdo

eye-flower: (l.837) could be either of two common wildflowers, eyebright (euphrasia) or daisy (day's eye)

When Browning was very old, he was asked what was meant to happen at the end of 'In a Balcony'. He thought that Norbert would not be executed, but that the Queen would die of a broken heart (or shock!). However, as is usual in Browning's work, it is not what happens but what is said that matters. This version of the eternal triangle is full of conflicting noble passions which have a way of revealing the selfishness of the protagonists. It is hard to believe Norbert will settle quietly down with Constance after this!

Saul

This poem is based on the characters of King Saul and David from the Bible, the First Book of Samuel. The speaker is David, who tells Abner about his struggle with the spirit which has possessed and nearly destroyed Saul. He began by playing music to Saul made up of the everyday melodies of his people, and Saul gave a sign of life but no more. Then David sang the praises of Saul himself, and slowly the King moved and folded his arms like a mountain shrugging off the last of winter's snow. But now Saul was listening, what should David sing? He loosed his imagination and sang of the meaning he saw in life itself, and of futurity when Saul's greatness will be acknowledged everywhere. David feels God was with him when he sang, giving him power to see into unknown mysteries. Now, talking to Abner, he can hardly believe the revelations himself. Saul moved away from the tent prop and sat towering over David as he sang, and David was filled with intense love for Saul. This love inspired his most revelatory song. Without the harp, he sang of God's love surrounding all creation, as he realised that God judges a man's intentions above his actions. David's surge of love for Saul – powerless in itself – has been made potent by God to help Saul. Even the weaknesses of mankind have value to God. David prophesies the coming of Christ to embody God's love in human flesh. In the ecstasy of this vision David left Saul and plunged through the streets of Jerusalem like a bearer of welcome news. Even the earth and the stars seemed ecstatic. Gradually his disorientated senses returned and he was left with an intense perception of meaning in the wilderness where he had sought refuge. The whole of nature seems to acknowledge the new law of faith which has been revealed to him, the human quality of God's love.

NOTES AND GLOSSARY:
Browning published the first nine sections of 'Saul' in 1845 with a note to indicate the poem was unfinished, and he completed it for *Men and Women*. The poem's two main sources are the *Bible* (I Samuel 16:14–23) and the 'Song of David' by the eighteenth-century poet, Christopher Smart (1722–71).

Abner:	(l.1) a captain in Saul's army (see the Bible, I Samuel 17:55)
the King:	(l.5) Saul was the first king of the Israelites
Saul and the spirit:	(l.9) from I Samuel 16:14–23
foldskirts:	(l.20) flysheets of the tent
king-serpent:	(l.31) the snake is undergoing the change of his skin
jerboa:	(l.45) a small African rodent which can leap remarkably

Levites:	(l.60) men from the tribe of Levi who assisted the priests
male:	(l.65) brilliant
a throe:	(l.93) the comparison is with childbirth
arrowy summons:	(l.104) shafts of spring sunshine which loosen the snow
ardours:	(l.115) fierce heats (also used of emotions)
Base with base:	(l.126) the bases of the hills appear to 'knit' together in the fading evening light
inconscious:	(l.162) unknowing
Carouse:	(l.171) drink deeply
seer:	(l.176) visionary, prophet
paper-reeds:	(l.188) papyrus reeds from which paper was made
evanish:	(l.202) die away, disappear
Hebron:	(l.203) a mountain south of Jerusalem
Kidron:	(l.204) a stream which flows by Hebron
error:	(l.213) Saul had neglected a sacrifice to the Lord (I Samuel 15:10–31)
solace:	(l.226) consolation
obeisance:	(l.254) humble bow
in abeyance:	(l.258) suspended, kept in readiness
wot:	(l.259) know
dower:	(l.272) gift or talent
Sabaoth:	(l.291) hosts of God (his armies)
impuissance:	(l.294) powerlessness
cohorts:	(l.314) bands of people (can be used of soldiers)
pent:	(l.320) imprisoned
behest:	command

---

36.   'De Gustibus—'

This poem is about contrasting tastes. The speaker begins by describing his friend's taste for the English countryside. He imagines his ghost will haunt an English lane, genially observing the courting couple in the grove of hazel trees. He pictures the ghost even moving away from the moonlight so as not to disturb them, knowing their season of love is as brief as the summer itself. In contrast with this picture, the speaker now describes his own taste in landscape. He likes the romance of the Italian mountains. His ghost may be found, if his friend looks, somewhere near a house by the sea further south in Italy, still appreciating the wide blue sea on the one hand and the crumbling paintings on the villa wall on the other. He pictures a girl bringing melons and news of a political shooting in the cause of Italian freedom. 'Italy' must be written on his heart, he conceives.

NOTES AND GLOSSARY:
Contrast forms not just the basis, but the whole point, of this poem. It is natural enough for the speaker to give his own taste more lines than his friend's, but the whole piece is delightfully free from all invidious qualities.

De Gustibus:	(*Latin*) concerning taste. The whole quotation is *De gustibus non est disputandum* – there can be no argument about taste
coppice:	a small grove of trees
Appenine:	the Appenines are a range of mountains in central Italy
land of lands:	Italy
cicalas:	insects which sing loudly all summer
drouth:	thirst
king:	Ferdinand II of Sicily (see notes on 'Old Pictures in Florence')
liver-wing:	right arm
Bourbon:	the name of King Ferdinand's family
Queen Mary's saying:	Mary Tudor is supposed to have said: 'When I am dead and opened, you shall find "Calais" lying in my heart'
she:	Italy

37. Women and Roses

The speaker is interpreting his dream about a symbolic red rose-tree. First he describes the tree which bears three blooms. Each is surrounded by a ring of dancing women. The first flower is circled by women out of history and art; the second by living women; and the third by women of the future. Yet they all dance in time to the same music.

The first rose is dealt with in stanzas 3 and 4. The flower is overblown, but the pale, imaginary women, who circle it, fire the speaker with the desire to record their vanished beauty in art. The second rose, ringed by contemporary beauties, is still full of nectar and the women who circle it rouse a passion in the speaker like that of the bee enveloped in the rich depths of a hyacinth. The imagery for these living women is richly sexual, but it is only his 'dream' and the women ignore him and go on circling their rose. In the last two stanzas, the speaker concentrates on the rosebud which symbolises the next crop of female beauty for him. He hopes these future lovelies may inspire him to create, as an artist, another woman ('an Eve'). But as before, these women too ignore the speaker and just contemplate their own rose, the symbol of their own being, regardless of their worshipper, lover or creator.

NOTES AND GLOSSARY:

cadence:	measured movement, rhythm
unimpeached:	unentangled, unhurt
fix you, fire you, freeze you:	methods of making them into works of art. (All puns: *fix* – to make a colour fast or to attract someone's eye; *fire* – to bake a clay statue or inspire a feeling; *freeze* – to paralyse, but also a pun on 'frieze')
plinth:	the base of a statue or column. The lines could be paraphrased 'just as deep as the bee drops from the statue's plinth to be sucked in by the hyacinth, so (deep) will I bury me . . .'
cincture:	belt or girdle

---

38. Protus

The speaker is visiting a museum full of statues of Roman Emperors. He first describes this Child-Emperor, Protus, and reads out what his guidebook says about him. He became Emperor while he was a baby, and his babyish gestures ruled the Empire. Artists carved him and wise old men tried to write their learned books in simple style for him, so he could grow into a good man to rule his people. At this point the speaker turns the page and is shocked to find no more about Protus, but a note on the next Emperor, John the Pannonian. This illegitimate son of an illiterate smith seized power and ruled for six years until he was poisoned by one of his own sons. The guidebook has a footnote about him saying that John may have let Protus escape to a Northern province and become a stable hand who wrote a book 'on worming dogs', or perhaps to Thrace where there was an aged monk called Protus. The speaker, who so relished the bust of the baby, barely glances at the bust of the brutal John.

NOTES AND GLOSSARY:

Browning invented both these Emperors as examples of the decayed days of the Roman Empire.

Half emperors and quarter emperors:	there were two or more emperors at this stage of the Empire (after 285 AD)
fillet:	headband
Loric:	corselet/cuirass (breastplate of Roman armour)
a god:	Augustus was made a god in 14AD
porphyry:	a hard, beautifully coloured stone
Byzant:	Byzantium, the capital of the Roman Empire after 300AD
whoso:	whoever

John the Pannonian: Pannonia was a northern Roman province
Huns: fierce enemies of Rome in the fourth and fifth centuries AD
hunting-stables: Pannonia was renowned for its hunting dogs
Thrace: a Roman province in the Balkans
griped: pinched

---

39. Holy-Cross Day

The Jew who speaks here is being deliberately irreverent as he sneeringly invites his friends to Church. He is noisy when the Bishop enters to preach and he mocks the Christian ritual. He turns to the twelve Jews who have been chosen for 'conversion' – five are thieves who deserve this as a punishment and seven are beggars who will no doubt be given Christian charity. They all pretend to be impressed by the sermon, but cannot credit the condemnation of usury since the Bishop himself borrows money from them. Thus the Jews lend money to pay for Christian vices, and in return the Christians try to force their virtues on the Jews! While the twelve 'converts' go up, the rest of the Jews recite their own prayers under their breath and the speaker recalls the Song of Death of Rabbi ben Ezra which offers the hope that the oppression of the Jews will end and their Messiah come. The speaker thinks that Jesus himself would be on the Jews' side at this hypocritical Holy-Cross Day sermon. At least the Jews now reject Barabbas as they then rejected Christ, whereas the Christians behave like Barabbas while professing Christ. The Jews' refusal to be converted to this degraded form of Christianity would be seen as honourable, and help to bring them finally to the Promised Land.

NOTES AND GLOSSARY:
The 'quotation' from the *Diary by the Bishop's Secretary, 1600* was written by Browning himself. The 'crumb' to 'dogs' reference is to the Bible, Matthew 15:26–7, and the reference which underlies the whole piece is from Luke 14:23 – 'Compel them to come in.'

Holy-Cross Day: the fourteenth of September
to handsel: to inaugurate
acorned: full of acorns, which are what hogs eat
bloom: complexion
chine: backbone (the boy has his back to the congregation)
laps: dewlaps, hanging folds of skin
quotha: indeed! (used contemptuously)
cog: cheat
cozen: deceive
mount to a Turk: Christians thought Jews were 'lower' than infidel

	Turks because the Jews were held responsible for the death of Christ
hanging-face:	the face of someone born to be hanged
worst of trades:	the Christian description of usury
Corso:	a main street in Rome
pricked:	spurred, urged
scapegoats:	those who bear the blame for the rest
Ben Ezra's Song of Death:	Rabbi ben Ezra was a Spanish Jew (1092–1167) and Browning wrote a poem under his character in *Dramatis Personae* (1864). The words in this poem were invented by Browning and are not ben Ezra's
watch and ward:	compare with 'watch and pray', the Bible, Mark 13:33
If thou wast He:	if Jesus was the Messiah
Barabbas:	Barabbas was condemned to be crucified along with Christ, but Pilate, the judge, asked the crowd of Jews which of them he should spare. The crowd chose Barabbas. See the Bible, John 18:40 and Luke 23:18–19
Rome:	the Roman Catholic Church
Calvary:	the place where Jesus was crucified
ghetto:	the Jewish quarter of the town, to which they were confined. ('Borghetto' is Italian for a little town)
The present Pope:	(Browning's note) Gregory XVI (1765–1846)

---

40. The Guardian-Angel: A Picture at Fano

This poem seems to be the only one Browning wrote in the three years following his marriage to Elizabeth Barrett and it has a pious tone which is far more common in her poetry than his. He admired her work and considered her the better poet, though she paid him the same compliment. They were staying at Ancona in July 1848 and visited Fano where they saw the painting by Guercino in the Church of San Agostino. It shows a child praying on a tomb and being guarded by a large angel.

The speaker in the poem begs the angel to come and guard him, and he will gaze at the angel's face while it puts his hands into an attitude of prayer. The next stanza is peculiarly uneasy in itself – the speaker seems to feel that the only way to find peace is to cover his eyes with the angel's hands, to be prevented from thinking and finally to be 'supprest' into quiet and tranquility. He hopes that this would lead him to a new view of the world where God's intentions would be clear to him, so that to realise the beauty of the world would be to love it, and the act of loving it would be the duty one had to God. As if feeling the mawkish cliché he has just uttered had better be justified than explained, the speaker now does two things: he attributes the sentimental 'meaning' to the picture rather than claiming it himself; and he makes the poem into part of a private address to an old friend of his, Alfred Domett, which has the effect of semi-excluding any other reader. He fills the scene in for Domett, describes the picture again and their three visits to it. He has just taken 'one thought' (maybe the Angel successfully 'supprest' the others) given him by the picture and has 'spread it out' into the poem. (The suggestion that Browning's poetry is, in any other poem in *Men and Women*, a 'spinning-out' of one single thought is risible!) Finally he escapes the angel altogether, wonders where Domett is now he has emigrated to New Zealand, and rounds off lamely with a geographical note ('This is Ancona, yonder is the sea').

NOTES AND GLOSSARY:
Browning's opinion of the picture changed: in 1883, he wrote, 'I probably saw the original picture in a favourable *darkness*; it was blackened by taper-smoke, and one fancied the angel all but surrounded with cloud . . .'

bird of God:	angel
Guercino:	Giovanni Francesco Barbieri (1591–1666) was a Bolognese painter
dear friend:	Alfred Domett, a friend of Browning's from about 1840. He emigrated to New Zealand in May 1842
My angel:	Mrs Browning
power/And glory:	this echoes the Lord's Prayer
Wairoa:	a river in New Zealand

---

41. Cleon

Cleon is writing to his Emperor, Protus (both invented by Browning), to thank him for the gifts he has sent and for his letter, honouring Cleon as an artist. In recognition of Protus's noble patronage, he will pray to Zeus for him. Cleon now tries to answer Protus's questions: he confirms that he created the poem, the song, the statue, the paintings, the theory, the philosophy and the new musical mode which Protus asks about. Modern artists can combine the achievements of their predecessors like a man making a chequered pavement. To support his claim that modern art is as great as, though more polyglot than, the art of the ancients, Cleon uses an analogy. He compares man's capacity for knowledge to a sphere. Each ancient artist took a single direct line to the limit of the sphere, but once that had been done, just a single drop of talent could touch the whole surface of the sphere by imitation. But the sphere is actually full of the 'subtler element' of air, which also surrounds the sphere itself, though common folk call it emptiness and ignore the finer qualities of their own souls. Cleon hopes that man will progress spiritually as well as materially; he himself may not be as great an artist in any single field as the ancients, but he surpasses them in being able to create art in many forms. The wild flower of ancient art may have been larger, but he has cultivated it.

Protus's second question is about how the ageing Cleon views death. His works will 'live' after him. But Cleon replies that age does not bring detachment, nor even spirituality, and the soul starves if it loses its joy in nature. But the spirit is still capable of being dissatisfied with itself, and Cleon almost wishes Zeus had left man soulless. There is no consolation in the thought that his works will 'live' after him, they seem rather to mock him. He gave his youth to perfecting his art to express the beautiful, but finds himself too old to enjoy it. You can't invite a poem to have a drink with you! Zeus has apparently made no arrangement for the immortal yearning in man's soul. So Cleon wishes Protus a long and happy life. In answer to the last question about the Christian preaching of Paul, which would seem to offer a spiritual prospect such as Cleon desires, Cleon feels that the barbarous doctrines of such uncivilised people as these 'could be held by no sane man'.

NOTES AND GLOSSARY:
The quotation at the head of the poem is from the Bible, Acts of the Apostles 17:28. Paul's preaching has probably prompted Protus to write.

poet:	(l.1) used to mean any artist
isles:	(l.1) Sporades, part of Greece
in his Tyranny:	(l.4) in his power (not used derogatorily)
unlades:	(l.7) unloads
portico:	(l.9) colonnade, porch
libation:	(l.38) a drink-offering to gods
Zeus:	(l.41) the supreme god of the Greeks
epos:	(l.47) epic poem
plates:	(l.47) tablets
sun-god:	(l.51) a statue of Apollo on the lighthouse
Poecile:	(l.53) a colonnade in the market place in Athens covered in paintings
moods:	(l.60) musical modes or scales
drupe:	(l.132) a primitive wild plum
Homer:	(l.139) author of the Greek epic poems *The Iliad* and *The Odyssey*
Terpander:	(l.140) the founder of Greek music
Phidias:	(l.141) Greek sculptor and painter (c.500–c.432BC)
his friend:	(l.141) Pericles, Athenian statesman (c.500–429BC)

inconscious:	(l.226) unknowing
clombst:	(l.243) climbed
It skills not:	(l.249) it is no use
Naiad:	(l.252) a Greek water-nymph (in this case, a statue)
Phoebus:	(l.288) Apollo, Greek god of the sun, art, and healing
Sappho:	(l.304) a Greek poetess of the seventh century BC
Aeschylus:	(l.305) a Greek tragedian (525–456BC)
fly:	(l.332) butterfly, a symbol for the soul
Paulus:	(l.340) the Apostle Paul
Christus:	(l.341) Jesus Christ

42. The Twins

Browning has taken the story of this poem from Martin Luther's *Table Talk*, which was translated into English by William Hazlitt (1778–1830). 'Date' and 'Dabitur' come from the Bible, Luke 6:38.

The poet begins by introducing Luther's fable, saying that Luther seemed to blossom with tales as a gorse bush flowers – the rougher the stories, the better for his purposes, since they stick better than smooth ones. This fable tells how a beggar asked for charity at an Abbey, but the Abbot replied they were too poor to give because none gave to them. But the beggar reminded him that the Abbey had once housed a pair of twins, called Date (Give) and Dabitur (It shall be given unto you). If one were well, the other throve, but if one ailed, so did his brother. Thus the way to help one was to help the other, for they supported each other. The only danger would be of a relapse! The Abbot is chastened by this tale. Luther ends by hinting that the beggar was an angel.

NOTES AND GLOSSARY:
This poem was first published in 1854 for a charity, 'Refuge for Young Destitute Girls'.

Luther:	Martin Luther (1483–1546), a German theologian, began the Reformation
furze:	gorse (very prickly, and flowers all year)
uncouther:	rougher, more rugged
lenten:	dismal

43. Popularity

This poem is in two parts, the first indicating the reward that God will give the unpopular poet and the second describing by analogy the growing recognition of the poet's talent after his death, and the way imitators make themselves rich and famous by plagiarising him.

The speaker sets out to give us a portait of the 'true poet' because he might die at any time. He recognised the poet's greatness, and that he was really 'a star' and not a mere glow-worm. God, he believes, will let the poet shine out in the end so that future people will honour him in spite of current neglect. In the meantime, the speaker is describing the poet as he is now, unregarded. He is like a fisherman on the beach of the ancient city of Tyre who fished up the shells from which the royal blue dye can be made. Soon everyone knew about the dye, but at that moment it was just a possibility in the rough net of the fisherman, mere shells, useless until the skilled artist refined their colour out. Then, the dye becomes a commercial proposition – all the literary imitators use the true poet's discovery and become popular, rich and fat. The speaker indignantly asks: But who discovered the wonderful thing in the first place? What kind of reward did the true poet get?

NOTES AND GLOSSARY:
In spite of some critical disagreement, probably the most straightforward interpretation of the reference to John Keats (1795–1821) at the end of this poem is that he was meant as the 'true poet'. The image of the blue dye may well refer to an untitled sonnet by Keats, written on 8 February 1818, which begins 'Blue! 'Tis the life of Heaven . . .'

chalice:	goblet
Tyre:	the ancient Phoenician port south-west of Beirut
Tyrian shells:	the Phoenicians used the royal blue dye which comes from the whelk which lives in the murex shell
Astarte:	the Phoenician goddess of Love
sublimed:	made sublime, exalted
pall:	cloak of office
Solomon:	biblical King of All Israel
Spouse:	Solomon married the Pharaoh of Egypt's daughter
warp or woof:	threads in weaving
Hobbs, Nobbs, Stokes and Nokes:	imaginary imitators of the true poet
line:	a pun on a line in painting, poetry or music *or* the journalist's lines for which he is paid by numbers
gorge:	feed greedily
murex:	see note above on 'Tyrian shells'

---

44. The Heretic's Tragedy: A Middle-Age Interlude

This extraordinary poem is modelled on the sixteenth-century interludes which were usually farces. Master Gysbrecht was invented by Browning. In spite of the grisly subject-matter, the poem is jocular and grotesquely cheerful in tone, perhaps influenced by the bizarrely comical, though terrifying, medieval pictures by such artists as Bosch or Breughel.

The Interlude opens with the Abbot's stern words regarding the Justice of God, which are underlined by a plagal cadence on the organ. One singer tells the tale of John's trial. Then the Interlude moves to the place of execution. John is tied above the pile of sticks, his executioners spit in his face and leap back as the fire is lit, and they praise God. The singer then mocks the man who is being burned alive, saying that if he called for Christ's help he would just be reminded how he has abused Christ's name before. Then in rhetorical questions, the singer accuses John of ignoring the menace of Justice and believing God was only Love, like an eternal rose. The singer exposes John's lack of chastity, and the contempt he had for Divine Justice. The singer rises to a climax in describing the burning body of the heretic like a great rose of Sharon, bursting with sparks like the stamens of that flower, transpiring blood like dew, and reeking of sulphur to mark his passage to Hell. The singer concludes with John's final terrifying vision of the Name and Face of Christ, whom he has abused, as his Judge. The sight convulses him and, with a final choking cry, he dies. The Abbot then reasserts the Infinite Mercy mentioned at the beginning by praying for all lost souls.

NOTES AND GLOSSARY:
The tone of this poem is its most challenging feature, but it is not unknown for Browning to use the technique of making grim comedy far more striking than a solemn account of the events could be.

Rosa mundi . . .:	(*Latin*) Rose of the World, support me with flowers
conceit:	idea, fancy
Cantuque . . .:	and a Virgil in songs
Hock-tide:	holidays, the second Monday and Tuesday after Easter
Gavisus eram:	(*Latin*) I had rejoiced
Jessides:	son of Jesse (David). This piece of garbled Latin imitates Psalm 122
I wis:	I know
John:	Jacques du Bourg-Molay, Grand Master of the Knights Templar, who gained wealth by going on Crusades. They were disbanded by Philip IV of France, and Jacques was imprisoned, tortured and forced to confess before being burned at the stake in March 1314
Aldabrod:	the name seems to have been invented by Browning; an infidel
Saladin:	a Turkish king who fought against the Crusaders. Master Gysbrecht's dates are wrong, though, since he died fifty years before Jacques du Bourg-Molay was born

clavithern:	an early form of keyboard instrument
tumbrils:	open carts
bavins:	bundles of brushwood
Billets:	short, thick sticks
chafe:	rage (also means sore)
Laudes:	(*Latin*) psalms of praise
Laus Deo:	(*Latin*) praise God
Salva reverentia:	(*Latin*) a saving reverence is called to make the congregation kneel
Sharon's rose:	Sharon's rose is mentioned in the Bible, Song of Solomon 2:1, as a symbol of love
leman:	lover
Anther:	the part of the stamen of a flower which bears the pollen

---

45. Two in the Campagna

The speaker is roaming the Campagna with his mistress on a fine May day, and they have sat down to appreciate the landscape. He describes his thoughts, which are like the spiders' webs drifting across their path. He tries to follow one particular strand of thought. Like the web, which leads first to a flower and then on all over the slope where they sit, his thought is hard to follow. His eye moves over the beautiful plain and the whole landscape seems imbued with their love – 'silence and passion, joy and peace'. Here nature lies exposed to the eye of heaven. Why can't they be as frank? Impulsively, he gives vent to his oddly incongruous and painful thought, mentioned vaguely (stanza 2), that love is not under one's control. He would like to make his mistress his whole world, but he knows it is impossible. Momentarily he can do it, but 'then the good minute goes'. He is like mere thistledown, not like the classical lover whose emotions are 'fixed'. On the very verge of realising how to love, he none the less misses it – all the he learns is the limitations of the human heart.

NOTES AND GLOSSARY:

Campagna:	the grassy plain south-east of Rome, subject of many romantic paintings as the ruins conveniently enhance the quality of the landscape
weft:	web
honey-meal:	pollen
champaign:	(*French*) plain (Campagna)
good and ill:	this echoes the marriage service 'for better for worse'
Fixed:	refers to Shakespeare's sonnet 116 ('an ever-fixed mark')

46. A Grammarian's Funeral

The speaker here is one of the dead Grammarian's pupils who sings the poem to accompany the coffin to its final resting-place, up in the city in the mountains away from the lower plains where he lived. The speaker praises his dead master for his lifelong devotion to studying obscure points of grammar from old manuscripts, his determination to 'know all' before he would take any pleasure in life.

The procession goes from the low villages up to the city fortress, and finally to the city market-place as the speaker celebrates the Grammarian's faith that 'Man has forever' and only animals need to live for the present (an ironic claim at a funeral, perhaps, though the speaker does not intend irony). Regardless of his own physical decay, the Grammarian worked fiercely as if his trust were in fame after his death, not in life. Where ordinary men can achieve the low ideals they set themselves in life, the Grammarian's ideals were so high that he had to trust in God for his reward. Even as he was dying, he sorted out the obscure particles of Greek grammar.

They place the coffin on the funerary platform just as the clouds noticed earlier break into a thunderstorm, which the speaker feels adds a suitably sublime touch to the funeral. Then they leave the Grammarian to his obscure dignity, unrecognised by 'the world' both in his life and in his death.

NOTES AND GLOSSARY:

crofts:	smallholdings, farms
thorpes:	villages, hamlets
Chafes:	grows heated (smokes)
censer:	incense-burner
sepulture:	burial
citadel:	fortress guarding a city
warning:	summons
Apollo:	the Greek god of the Arts who played a lyre
gowned:	wore a gown, that is, became a scholar
crabbed:	intricate, difficult
Prate:	chatter foolishly
queasy:	sick
spurned:	rejected
peculiar:	individual, special to him
Calculus:	(*Latin*) the stone (gallstones)
dross:	rubbish
Tussis:	(*Latin*) the cough (bronchitis)
hydroptic:	terribly thirsty
rattle:	death rattle

Hoti, Oun, De: Greek particles meaning 'that', 'then', and 'towards'. In a letter to Tennyson in 1863, Browning wrote that the Grammarian was working on 'the biggest of the littlenesses'
purlieus: the borders or edges
not to Live but Know: compare with 'Cleon', lines 310–18

---

47. One Way of Love and **48. Another Way of Love**

Here a male and female speaker are contrasted. The man in the first poem is humility personified and never complains if his beloved Pauline just brushes his attentions aside and drops his roses in the dirt. He spends ages learning to play the lute but expects her to reject his music. If so, he'll give it up, just remembering his hope. He has trained himself to be a lover, and the test is whether Pauline will accept him. But again, he almost expects rejection: he can take it! (The reader may feel that if she were ever nice to him he would die of shock.)

On the other hand, the lady speaker in 'Another Way of Love' is being rejected by her lover, who is tired of her 'serene deadness' and perpetual good temper. Like a rose-tree, she will 'mend' the gaps he made in her heart and repair her self-respect. In fact, she will probably flower more fully and find another man who appreciates her better. Or else she may use an unexpected flash of temper to rid herself of creepy-crawly men altogether – she will have to consider which method to adopt.

The beauty of both poems lies in the way both speakers conduct their defences. The first, the man, expecting rejection, would win if Pauline accepted him but is still proved right if she rejects him. The second speaker, the woman, plays the man's insincere game back at him. We seem to gain insight into both their relationships, though their lovers never speak, and we sense that neither is quite the defenceless victim that their ideas of 'love' might suggest.

NOTES AND GLOSSARY:
Another Way of Love
clear scores: settle accounts (with you)
Eadem semper: (*Latin*) always the same
refulgent: gloriously bright, shining
June-lightning: refers to the superstition that summer lightning can get rid of insects
film-work: cobwebs (in the 1855 and 1863 editions, 'spinning')

---

49. 'Transcendentalism: A Poem in Twelve Books'

The speaker is a poet who is being subjected to a reading of the poem in the title. He begs the transcendental poet to stop and listen to him, criticising the prosy, abstract ideas and lack of colour and music in the work. Ideas can be put in prose. Perhaps the transcendentalist makes the mistake of thinking that 'adult' poetry is about ideas while colour and music are childish: but the speaker points out that these difficult abstract ideas take years to decipher. Poetry should conjure up a vision in a moment, and stock the reader's imaginative life. After this little lesson, the speaker patronisingly invites the transcendentalist to continue with his poem. The speaker will appreciate the 'poetry' of his effort even though his poem is rubbish; and he settles back to enjoy the sight of the innocent cherub-like transcendental poet earnestly reciting.

NOTES AND GLOSSARY:
This poem is a comparison between two types of poetry. The speaker's own poem (what we read) follows his theory of lyric poetry, and attempts vividness in preference to argument. Browning deliberately makes his argument a bit second-hand so that the attack he makes on the transcendental poet tells us much about his own verse.

brother:	the speaker is a poet too
prolusion:	preliminary essay
Swiss tube:	alpenhorn (alphorn)
Swedish Boehme:	(changed to 'German Boehme' from 1868) Jacob Boehme (1575–1624), German mystic and follower of Paracelsus, about whom Browning had written a long poem. Emanuel Swedenborg (1688–1772), the Swedish mystical philosopher, mentions him too, and he was a favourite of EBB's
daisy:	the name derives from 'day's eye'
colloquized:	conversed
tough book:	perhaps Boehme's *De Signatura Rerum* (1622) ('Concerning the Significance of Things')
emendating:	correcting, removing errors
mage:	magician, learned man
John of Halberstadt:	Johannes Teutonicus, a fifteenth-century German wise-man
vents:	gives vent to
brace:	pair
finer chords:	the high-pitched strings of the harp are thinner than those of lower pitch, and nearer the harpist's head

50. Misconceptions

In this poem the contrast which gives rise to wryly ironic reflections in the reader's mind is contained in each of the stanzas. The first stanza points out the particular branch low down on the tree which the Bird just perched upon before going higher to build her nest. The branch blossomed with pleasure to think the Bird might have chosen it to build upon – which, of course, she had not done.

Similarly, in the second stanza, the poor courtier is pointed out, who happened to be at hand when the Queen felt a bit faint and had to lean on the first thing near. The Queen has since married a King, of course – but just for a moment, the courtier was thrilled to hold her like a lover who would be permitted to serve her with his heart.

NOTES AND GLOSSARY:
regal dalmatic: a king's coronation robe

---

51.   One Word More: To EBB

This poem is the only one in *Men and Women* where Browning frankly addresses his wife (Elizabeth Barrett Browning or EBB), and it dedicates the fifty poems to her. The title may be a reference to a phrase in a letter she wrote to him before they were married, where she forbade him to mention love and marriage to her: 'We must leave this subject – and I must trust you to leave it without one word more.'

The poem was written in London while Browning was seeing the other poems in the collection through the press. Browning dated the manuscript 22 September 1855. In every edition after EBB's death in 1861, Browning had his initials (RB) placed at the end of this poem by way of signature. The whole poem is written in trochaic pentameters, the only extended use of this metre in Browning's work and another aspect of the uniqueness of this poem.

The poet opens with the dedication of *Men and Women* to his wife, asking her to accept not only his love, but his work also. He reminds her of the hundred sonnets which the painter, Raphael, wrote for his mistress, using a pencil he only used to draw pictures of the Virgin Mary. His pictures of the Virgin were for the public, but his sonnets were exclusively for his lover. The poet knows that he and EBB, being lovers, would prefer to see Raphael's private sonnets than go and stare at his public Madonnas, but the book is lost. Then Browning tells how Dante once set out to paint a picture of an angel for his mistress, Beatrice, but was interrupted by Florentine officials who arrested him. Browning and EBB would rather see that painting than read a new poem by Dante, but this is impossible and the lovers and Beatrice 'bear the loss' of the picture 'forever'. Browning believes that every artist wishes to create one work for his lover that will express him, not in the public way that his other works do, but with unique frankness. He says that if they could do this one thing, they would willingly give up the art they practise – the painter would prefer to write poetry and the poet to paint – to express their real selves to their beloveds.

Why should artists feel like this? Browning answers his own question by saying that the heavenly gift of talent is diminished or modified by the way it is used. Even Moses, who drew water from rock, must have remembered bitterly how his people had first mocked him and then failed to thank him for the water. Memories like this can make the practice of art bitter to the artist, who seems to be facing his critics again as he works. He dare not be himself, but has to regard his audience. If Moses had loved only one woman, either his wife or his concubine, he would have preferred to be her camel who could just die faithfully for her, rather than that complicated being, a prophet!

Browning realises that he will never be able to paint pictures or carve statues or write music for EBB, so all he has to offer her is his poetry. He asks her to look carefully at his work for hints of the private within the public poem. She has known him as he wrote all the poems, bringing each character to life; in this last poem he speaks for himself. He asks her to see beyond the 'poor' words and into the expressive method used throughout his work. But then he realises that she *does* know him. Together they saw the moon in Florence which now shines on them in London. He recalls the myth of Endymion, the mortal man loved by the moon goddess, and he thinks she must have shown him her hidden side. Nobody has ever seen the dark side of the moon. Even the most ordinary of men, like the moon, has two sides – one for facing the world, and the other to show only to his lover. Though he is talking of himself, Browning realises that this is also true of EBB herself, who is a poet in the world's eyes, but 'the best' side of her is given to him as his wife. From this wonderful revelation of her hidden side he is able to understand what Raphael's sonnets or Dante's picture must have been like.

NOTES AND GLOSSARY:

Sonnets:	Baldinucci mentioned Raphael's sonnets in his *Notizie*
his lady:	both Vasari and Baldinucci say Raphael had a mistress
San Sisto:	Sistine Madonna, a picture in Dresden
Foligno:	*Madonna di Foligno*, in the Vatican
Florence:	*Madonna del Granduco,* in the Pitti Palace, Florence
Louvre:	*La Belle Jardinière,* in the Louvre, Paris
Guido Reni:	the Bolognese painter (1575–1642)
Bice:	short for Beatrice
He who:	Moses's deeds are in the Bible, Exodus 17:6 and Numbers 20:11
O'er-importuned:	over-pressing, too solicitous
phalanxed:	drawn up in ranks like soldiers

Jethro's daughter: Zipporah the wife of Moses; his concubine was an Ethiopian bond slave

missal-marge: the margin of the pages of a prayer book

Karshook: changed to Karshish after 1872

thrice-transfigured: the moon is in its last quarter, so it changed three times before this

imbrued: stained

Fiesole: a village outside Florence

Samminiato: San Miniato, a church outside Florence

a mortal: this refers to the story of Endymion who was loved by Diana, the goddess of the moon

mythos: myth

Zoroaster: also called Zarathustra, a sixth-century BC mystic and astronomer

Galileo: Galileo Galilei (1564–1642), the astronomer, he invented the telescope

Homer: the Greek poet who wrote a hymn to the moon which was translated by Shelley

Keats: John Keats (1795–1821) wrote a long poem about Endymion

sapphire: this vision is recorded in the Bible, Exodus 24:9–11

Part 3

Commentary

The dramatic monologue

'My poetry is far from "the completest expression of my being".'
(Letter to Elizabeth Barrett, 1846)

Browning did not invent the form of the dramatic monologue, but he did develop it to such an extent that it is hard to consider the form without thinking of his particular use of it. Almost all of Browning's poems are dramatic monologues. The essential quality of this form is that the speaker in the poem is projected as a character distinct from the poet himself. The speaker, for instance, usually has a specific intention in his monologue which is not shared by the poet: Fra Lippo Lippi is trying to avoid arrest, so he explains his case to the guards and this forms the poem; Karshish is writing to his colleague, Abib, about a medical case which interests him, and his letter forms the poem. Clearly Browning does not share these characters' initial intentions. Furthermore, he often makes his speakers address particular listeners and not the reader directly. Bishop Blougram (apparently pronounced 'Blogram' by Browning) is addressing the journalist, Gigadibs; Andrea del Sarto is talking to his wife; in the poem 'Saul', David is addressing Abner. This means that the reader is not being directly appealed to in the monologue, but is in a detached position comparable to that of an audience. It is easy to see why the word 'dramatic' should be used to qualify 'monologue', in spite of the lack of action in all the poems.

The word 'dramatic' was used by Browning throughout his career to express his insistence that his poems were not about himself in any ordinary sense. For example, he wrote in 1867 that his poetry was 'always dramatic in principle, and so many utterances of so many imaginary persons, not mine'. He makes it plain that he consciously intended his poems to be objective pieces, and not exercises in self-expression. This is a deliberately unromantic stance and the monologues which he wrote are much more ironic and even comical than most romantic poetry.

Browning himself expressed his sense of the distinction between dramatic, objective work and romantic, subjective work in his *Essay on Shelley* (1852) which was written in the same period of his life as many of the poems in *Men and Women* (1855). In this essay*, he describes the objective poet as 'the fashioner; and the thing fashioned will of necessity be substantive, projected from himself and distinct'. He uses the example of Shakespeare as an 'objective' poet, so we can see the intimate connection in Browning's mind between objective poetry and dramatic form. Of the 'subjective poet' on the other hand, he says that 'he is impelled to embody the thing he perceives'. He calls him 'rather a seer than a fashioner, and what he produces will be less a work than an effluence'.

Thus we can see that, at the time when he was writing the poems in *Men and Women*, Browning was consciously distinguishing his own method of writing from that of the subjective or romantic poets such as Shelley, and was in fact making a deliberate claim for the unfashionable 'objective' method:

> It would be idle to inquire, of these two kinds of poetic faculty in operation, which is the higher or even rarer endowment. If the subjective might seem to be the ultimate requirement of every age, the objective, in the strictest state, must still retain its original value. For it is with this world, as starting point and basis alike, that we shall always have to concern ourselves; the world is not to be learned and thrown aside, but reverted to and re-learned.

We can see that Browning was considering the exact qualities of his own method and deliberately avoiding a more romantic one at the time when he was writing the *Men and Women* poems, but he used the word 'dramatic' to describe his work most of his life. The titles of some of his collections of poems show this: *Dramatic Lyrics*, 1842; *Dramatic Romances and Lyrics*, 1845; *Dramatis Personae*, 1864; and *Dramatic Idyls*, 1879, 1880.

It will naturally occur to you consequently to wonder what Browning's own plays were like, and some account of the way they fail to work may be of use. For instance, in his play called *A Blot in the 'Scutcheon* (1843), which Dickens admired, Browning creates a situation where the heroine, Mildred, has explained the reasons for her committing an unpardonable sin (sleeping with her fiancé before they marry) so touchingly and completely that it seems quite unnecessary of Browning to make her die as well! Absolutely nothing is gained by the action, precisely because the character's own words and feelings are so well portrayed: she does not need to die to move our compassion, and in fact the reverse happens – she loses it by overdoing the action. A brief comparison with the murderer who is the speaker in 'Porphyria's Lover'

---

* The quotations from it are taken from *Robert Browning: The Poems*, ed. John Pettigrew, 1981, vol.I., Appendix II, p.999.

will show how much more effective it can be to leave the audience to imagine such violent actions.

A 'dramatic monologue' in Browning's sense is not like a soliloquy in a play, nor like the romantic soul-searching of Byron in *Childe Harold*, of Shelley in his 'Stanzas Written in Dejection', or of Keats in his 'Ode to a Nightingale.' Its dramatic quality lies in its use of an objective character as speaker and in the fact that this objective speaker usually has particular reasons of his own for arguing the way he does. The reader is often almost eavesdropping on his arguments: the speaker is actually addressing some silent or even imaginary other person within the poem, and not the reader at all. The reader is consequently able to be detached in his assessment of the speaker's argument and to see the inherent ironies and contradictions which reveal his character and the real reasons why he speaks. Thus, for example, with Fra Lippo Lippi, there is an immediate need to talk his way out of being arrested, but the way in which he does this expresses his character – his dislike of the restraints imposed by the very organisation (the Church) which feeds him is mirrored in his anger at, and flattery of, the guards who have caught him; and both are expressive of the problem he faces in his painting of having to portray Saints but only liking and understanding real live people. The discipline and the spontaneity in him pull two ways. And since the point of these poems is always expressed in terms of one particular character, it will be plain why they have to be monologues and not conversations. Even the brief play, 'In a Balcony', has not one convincing action in it, but has just three fascinating characters who never understand a quarter as much about each other as the reader does about them all.

The first thing, then, to look for in every one of the poems is the central motive (or basic character, or the character's 'ruling passion' as Pope might have called it) of the speaker. Since we have only the speaker's word for everything within the poem, we need to look carefully not only at what he is saying but also at his manner of saying it. The one represents his intentions as he sees them, or his idea of himself, and the other is an involuntary revelation of himself. Neither alone would give us the true picture – it would be unjust to assess Lippo merely as a coward because he involuntarily reveals how intimidated he is by the guards in his fawning on them. He is much more than this: in his painting, his conviction about realism amounts to a kind of courage, opposing as it does the traditional ideas of his superiors. The lovers who speak in many of the poems are similarly complex, though most of them feel that their 'love' gives them extraordinary rights over their love-objects. The poet himself may well be critical of this. The conviction they all have is that love is in itself a good thing, and so in this confidence they reveal the passionate selfishnesses natural to their particular characters.

'Any Wife' is jealously demanding by temperament, whereas the woman who speaks in 'In a Year' is too self-sacrificial to be jealous. Each is distinct, endowed by Browning with a particular kind of character which reaches individuation in the situation he places it in. Even the speaker in 'By the Fire-side', which is surely the nearest Browning comes to self-revelation in *Men and Women*, is still a distinct, projected character, though he is given many of Browning's feelings and views, and a wonderful wife whose physique is very like Elizabeth Barrett's. None the less, neither here nor in 'One Word More' is Browning attempting self-portraiture: the speakers are *like* him, which is as good as saying that they are not actually him. The emotion in both poems deliberately excludes the reader from the private happiness of the speakers, just as much as Karshish's letter addresses Abib, not us. The poetry is still objective.

You will probably have noticed on your first reading of *Men and Women* how often the poems open with an exclamation: 'Hist, but a word, fair and soft! . . .' begins the organist in 'Master Hugues of Saxe-Gotha'; 'Oh, what a dawn of day! . .' cries the lover in 'A Lovers' Quarrel'. These exclamations and emphatic expressions are used by Browning to achieve dramatic effects though they do not imitate ordinary speech patterns as such, which Browning considered to be out of place in poetry: 'The Sailor-language is good in its own way: but as wrongly used in Art as real clay and mud would be, if one plastered them in the foreground of a landscape . . .'* Not all the speakers in *Men and Women* are so emphatic, but usually the very first words of the poem give the reader a strong impression of the speaker's mood and character, and even of his motive for speaking. They all seem to be at moments of some pressure, when their situations call forth from them more than their habitual degree of concern. It is this combination of the situation and the character taken together which makes it possible for the speakers, momentarily, to reveal the truth about themselves, and it is *only* in this way that they interest us as readers. This point was well expressed by the Victorian critic, Walter Pater (1839–94) in an essay in *The Renaissance* (1873), where he stated that the characters

> are not intrinsically interesting; they begin to interest us only when thrown into a choice situation. But to discriminate that moment, to make it appreciable by us, that we may 'find' it, what a cobweb of allusions, what double and treble reflexions of the mind upon itself, what an artificial light is constructed and broken over the chosen situation; on how fine a needle's point that little world of passion is balanced! Yet, in spite of this intricacy, the poem has the clear ring of

---

* E. Kintner (ed.), *The Letters of Robert Browning and Elizabeth Barrett 1845–6*, Harvard University Press, Cambridge, Massachusetts, 1969, p.366.

74 · Commentary

a central motive. We receive from it the impression of one imaginative
tone, of a single creative act . . .*

Browning himself would have agreed with Pater, for he wrote to a friend
(19 November 1863), 'That critique was fair in giving the right key to my
poetry, in as much as it *is* meant to have "one central meaning, seen only
by reflexion in details" . . .'.† The intricate details through which the
'central meaning' or motive is conveyed can be either purely imaginative
or based on fact, and we find in *Men and Women* that some of the
speakers are historical, while some are invented by Browning. As
readers, however, this difference does not affect the way we are intended
to respond. Every speaker is trying to put his case in the most favourable
light, and like the true rhetoricians they are, they can often manipulate
our sympathies, or even convince us that they are right point-by-point in
their arguments. The reader requires no knowledge of Renaissance
painting to understand Andrea del Sarto's failure, nor of Baroque music
to know what the fugue in 'Master Hugues of Saxe-Gotha' was like. But
the cumulative effect of each speaker's poem is more objective than this.
We realise that every choice of a metaphor to express an idea actually
reveals the character as well as the idea. Bishop Blougram habitually
expresses spiritual ideas in materialistic metaphors, and the complacency
of his soul is revealed through his quite simple assumption that his
material wealth must be envied by Gigadibs. The reverse proves to be
the case, for at the end of the poem Gigadibs goes off to lead the simple
life. In giving the Bishop his head, Browning has allowed him to damn
himself out of his own mouth. The art of reading such a poem is the art
of being a good listener. Whether we finally agree with the speaker or
not is up to us, but out first need is to hear him attentively. It is as if the
primary concern of this poetry is not to tell us what to think, but how to;
not to convey a particular philosophical truth, but the method by which
such truth is to be apprehended. In fact, in his greatest poem, *The Ring
and the Book* (1868), Browning does for once step out from his dramatic
characters at the end and in his own voice as the poet says:

It is the glory and the good of Art
That Art remains the one way possible
Of speaking truth, to mouths like mine at least . . .
(*The Ring and the Book*, Book XII)

An examination of the concluding poem in *Men and Women*, 'One
Word More', would reveal a similar idea of Art, though expressed by
means of a very different mood and situation. In this poem, Browning is
dedicating the volume of poems to his wife, and yet the whole point of

* W. Pater, *The Renaissance*, Fontana Library, Collins, London, 1961, p.206.
† A. J. Armstrong (ed.), *Letters of Robert Browning to Miss Blagden*, Baylor University
Press, Waco, Texas, 1923, p.101.

the poem is to say that he has no 'voice' of his own other than that of his 'Men and Women'. It is for this reason that he repeats the line: 'Where the heart lies, let the brain lie also' (lines 4 and 142). Effectively what is being said in both places is that he cannot and will not try to separate the 'truth' of what he is saying from his way of saying it, his 'Art'. In fact, it might almost be said that he objects to such a separation altogether and regards it as the root of bad poetry:

> All the bad poetry in the world . . . will be found to result from . . . a want of correspondency between [the] work and the verities of nature, – issuing in poetry . . . which shows a thing not as it is to mankind generally, nor as it is to the particular describer, but as it is supposed to be for some unreal, neutral mood . . .
>
> (from the *Essay on Shelley*)

By this definition, any poetry in which the words issue neither from a dramatically-imagined character nor from the poet himself, would have to be considered false. The quotation makes it plain that Browning's choice of the dramatic monologue form was not made in order to hide behind his characters while still making them say what he meant, but from the extraordinary conviction that his characters were the real 'poetry', and his role as poet was to mediate for them with words. The speaker in 'Transcendentalism' tells his brother poet: 'You are a poem, though your poem's naught.' And though he may be wrong to imagine that his own florid method could express the transcendentalist's ideas, he may none the less have a point. The necessity which the dramatic monologue embodies and which Browning embraces is that there can be as many views of the truth as there are people regarding it.

You may be feeling that all this is a way of covering-up for Browning – that his poems *must* express himself, and all the more so since he invented so many of his characters. You would be in good company if you did assume that, since a great many distinguished critics of Browning's work have done so. And it is obviously true that the poems in *Men and Women* relate to many aspects of Browning's own life. For example, he was himself involved in the most serious love-relationship of his life. He was fascinated by painting, quite apart from writing poetry about painters, and he was quite a skilled musician (or considered himself to be so at any rate). At the time he wrote the poems of *Men and Women* he was seriously re-thinking his own religious opinions, spurred on by Elizabeth Barrett Browning's intensely spiritual nature and by his grief over his mother's death in 1850. In some sense, these biographical facts do tell us why he wrote on some themes and not on others. But how does this help us to understand the poems themselves? We now have two characters to deal with instead of one, but only one of them is a work of art. What Browning means when he speaks of Art as being his means of 'speaking truth', is that only a work of art possesses the controlled clarity to be truly read by a detached other person. Thus only through his Art can he engage the reader's imagination, as opposed to relying on a possible interest in history, religion, politics, gossip, opinion, and so on; and by implication, only the imagination can grapple with this kind of 'truth' as opposed to mere facts. It seems that Browning is not seeking to hide behind his characters or using them to explore his own problems as such, but is actually unable to view himself imaginatively (as perhaps most of us are), and, recognising this, deliberately exercises that faculty on what are essentially all imaginary beings, as Shakespeare does.

If, then, we assume that Browning's reasons for writing almost exclusively in dramatic form are not to do with a desire to hide his own personality, but reflect a more positive artistic intention, we should still try to understand what those positive reasons were. First of all, a major influence on Browning's idea of Art must have been his father. The boy browsed freely through his father's large library and always regarded his father as having been the real source of his education. Now his father was a humorous caricaturist, a scholarly lover of the Classics and of the literature and painting of the eighteenth century. He even wrote a certain amount of rather jolly poetry himself, to amuse his own and other folk's children, including a 'Pied Piper of Hamelin' before his son wrote his famous poem on the same subject. The older Browning's drawings were usually character sketches, just showing a single figure or even a face with a characteristic expression, comically sketched. The affection he felt for Hogarth's works is obvious in his drawings. Browning's own drawings, the few that have survived, are very similar to his father's. They both reveal a fascination with character as such, and with what might be called in a more modern context, psychology. For instance, the older man was interested in the psychology of murder – the link with Browning's own greatest poem, *The Ring and the Book*, which he called a Roman Murder Story, will be obvious.

But it is not his father's taste alone which influenced Browning's choice: if it had been, perhaps his monologues would have been mere caricatures or sketches like his father's. Complementing this influence is the intense one of Browning's reading of the Romantic poets, especially Shelley and Byron, and to a lesser extent, William Wordsworth (1770–1850) and Keats as well. From this reading and his adolescent adoration of Shelley in particular was born a conception of the kind of poetry in which the speaker is not a mere mask for the poet but a passionate ego in itself, a complete character who is momentarily endowed by the poet with adequate language. It is as if in reading Byron and Shelley, Browning was illuminated by a sense of their conviction about themselves, rather than by their philosophies. His imitations of their styles in his earliest poetry are the logical beginnings for his later 'imitations' of all the characters he himself invented. Only in this way does he feel it is possible to study the depths of character, – or, to use his own words, 'the development of a soul'. Only if the character is brought to life as a convincing 'soul' or ego in itself, can this be achieved. He says, in the dedication to *Sordello* (1863), 'little else is worth study. I, at least, always thought so'.

Thus Browning's adoption and development of the form of the dramatic monologue can be seen to have been influenced by two completely different styles, which it is his strength as a poet to have forged into a single original style. He has united the objective, analytical idea of character from the eighteenth century – and from the classical authors such as Theophrastus (*c*.371–*c*.287BC), the pupil of Aristotle who wrote a series of 'Characters' – with the intense conviction of the Romantics, and the result is a host of astonishingly life-like and revealing 'Men and Women'.

Grouping the poems for commentary

The poems in *Men and Women* (1855) were not intended by Browning to be regarded as parts of a whole which had a particular significance achieved by the sum of these parts. This is obvious from the fact that he broke the collection up in 1863, leaving only eight of the original poems under the title of *Men and Women* and distributing the rest between *Dramatic Lyrics* and *Dramatic Romances*. (The exact division of the poems is given on pages 13–14.) It is also confirmed by the inclusion in *Men and Women* (1855) of poems such as 'The Twins' and 'Saul' which were written for quite other purposes (see the notes in Part 2 on these poems). We may safely say that the only real unity in the collection is provided by Browning's style and choice of the dramatic monologue form, and the fact that all the poems (except 'Saul') were written during a period of about six years up to the date of publication. There is no reason, therefore, to follow anyone's instincts except your own in dividing the poems up for commentary.

There are, however, some principles observed by Browning in his ordering of the poems which are worth consideration. For example, there are ironic reflections created by his putting 'A Lovers' Quarrel' straight after 'Love Among the Ruins' at the start of Volume I, and by following 'By the Fire-side' with 'Any Wife to Any Husband'. Furthermore, there are four pairs of poems which rely for their effect on the ironies created by reading both – 'Love in a Life' and 'Life in a Love'; 'Before' and 'After'; 'In Three Days' and 'In a Year'; and 'One Way of Love' and 'Another Way of Love'. Thus it would be foolish to ignore the existence of the collection when you single out some poems for comment. It might simply be said that the reading of all the fifty-one poems is like a lesson in how to read any one of them: without Lippo and Andrea, it would be hard to understand Cleon, but, conversely, he illuminates them too. Each of them is more difficult to understand out of the context of the rest.

There are, none the less, recurrent themes in *Men and Women* and probably the simplest grouping of the poems would follow them. For example, we could divide all the poems conveniently into four groups under general headings such as Love, Taste, Faith and Art (though you may disagree with these headings and/or the poems put under each):

Love

1. Love Among the Ruins
2. A Lovers' Quarrel
3. Evelyn Hope
5. A Woman's Last Word
8. By the Fire-side
9. Any Wife to Any Husband
11. Mesmerism
12. Serenade at the Villa
13. My Star
15. A Pretty Woman
17. Respectability
18. A Light Woman
19. The Statue and the Bust
20. Love in a Life
21. Life in a Love
23. The Last Ride Together
31. In Three Days
32. In a Year
34. In a Balcony
37. Women and Roses
45. Two in the Campagna
47. One Way of Love
48. Another Way of Love
50. Misconceptions
51. One Word More

Art – painting, music, poetry

6. Fra Lippo Lippi
7. A Toccata of Galuppi's

22. How it Strikes a Contemporary
25. Master Hugues of Saxe-Gotha
27. Memorabilia
28. Andrea del Sarto
33. Old Pictures in Florence
40. The Guardian-Angel
41. Cleon
43. Popularity
49. 'Transcendentalism'

Taste

4. Up at a Villa
14. Instans Tyrannus
26. Bishop Blougram's Apology
36. 'De Gustibus—'
38. Protus
46. The Grammarian's Funeral

Faith

10. An Epistle of Karshish
16. 'Childe Roland'
24. The Patriot
29. Before
30. After
35. Saul
39. Holy-Cross Day
42. The Twins
44. The Heretic's Tragedy

The largest group by far deals with Love (twenty-five poems) and it is fitting to point out here how original Browning is in his handling of this universal poetic theme. A glance down the list of poems under this head will make you realise that there is not a single poem where the reader is asked to make a hero (or heroine) of the lover who speaks. Some of the speakers are rather attractive – for instance, those in 'One Word More', 'By the Fire-side' and 'Two in the Campagna'; and some are downright repulsive – the speakers in 'Evelyn Hope' and 'Mesmerism', for example, seem repellent. But none of them is so admirable or so repulsive as to be considered either a hero or a villain. Furthermore, the love they express seems to be completely coloured by their own personalities. Instead of all partaking of a universal emotion and being transfigured by it, they seem to alter the nature of love itself by their examples of it. Thus, whilst love of some kind motivates the speaker in 'Serenade at the Villa', it would be most uncomfortable to have such a lover. In short, these poems rather destroy the idea that love (or any kind of feeling) is separable from the actual individual who feels it.

How then do you try to discuss the theme of love in these poems? The answer must follow Browning's hint in the ordering of the poems: by contrast and comparison. If you want to examine the speaker in 'A Woman's Last Word', you have lots of other ladies with whom to compare her. She has a good deal in common with the speaker in 'Any Wife to Any Husband', and some things in common with the speaker in 'In a Year'. By putting the three together, you will be able to see not only the three individual poems more clearly, but also the part of Browning's imagination which was engaged in realising his ideas about the woman's side of the issue.

All three ladies are essentially both loving and antagonistic towards their men, and embody a certain conflict within themselves which is surely characteristic of the complex and powerful emotion of love. In one sense, they show Browning re-examining the age-old Battle of the Sexes, but in another, they illuminate his revolutionary handling of character as such – that is, not just seen as a collection of traits and feelings in a particular conjunction like the pieces in a kaleidoscope, but fired with their own fierce egocentric uniqueness which makes even their most common emotions expressive of their peculiar individualities. Thus the aggressiveness of the speaker in 'A Woman's Last Word' is part of her love, and this comes out in her quarrelling, as she forcibly encounters her lover in her struggle to understand their relationship. But 'Any Wife' has a more submissive approach, even though she has an equal belief in her own rightness at her lover's expense. And in their own ways, both are meeting the problem which engages many of Browning's lovers, male and female: a disappointment in the reality of their own feelings, compared with their ideals of what those feelings should be and achieve. The speaker in 'Two in the Campagna' voices this aspect of love with most clarity, perhaps, but it is there in most of the lovers. The rider in 'The Last Ride Together' even makes this failure his glory, in order to enjoy the last moments of his mistress's company the more. In all these variations, some enchanting and some grotesque, it would be futile to deny that the only name for the emotion which drives them is still 'love'. In coming to understand the poems in this group, the reader will probably expand his own idea of 'love' too.

The smallest group of poems under the headings suggested above is also the vaguest, and 'Bishop Blougram's Apology' has been deliberately included here under *Taste* and not under *Faith* in order to make the importance of this group clear. In fact, it seems that the worthy Bishop never does reveal his faith to Gigadibs, nor to the reader, but instead argues that faith is an impossibility. His argument then rests on his deliberate choice of a style of existence which suits his image of his own importance on the one hand and his ornate Baroque taste on the other. However, since what is called here his 'taste' leads him very deeply into a controversy about the nature of faith, his inclusion under this heading is intended to emphasise that there is a profound expression of character in taste itself. The most transparent example of this is in 'De Gustibus', where the speaker simply contrasts the taste in landscape of his friend with his own, and the result is a delightful and quite amoral celebration of their differences as such. He likes his friend precisely because he is so different in taste. He knows himself better by contrast with his friend. Thus he naturally devotes more of the poem to himself, but puts his friend first.

'Up at a Villa – Down in the City' gives a more detailed exposition of the speaker's character, and we perceive qualities in him which we may or may not like, such as his gregariousness – he buttonholes his listener quite shamelessly, for instance. None the less, here again the major self-consciousness of the speaker is expressed in his preference for one style of living over another, and as a matter of taste rather than morality. In fact, with this monologue it would be pointless for the reader to decide, as the speaker does, that city life is preferable to country life or vice versa, because he would thereby miss the delicate irony of the speaker's position, which is that it *suits* him to parade his poverty and exile from city life. His imagination makes city life seem a constant series of events, far more interesting than it could be in fact. Similarly, his close observation of the despised countryside around the villa makes it plain that he doesn't actually find it so boring as he likes to make out. If the reader merely tried either to agree or disagree with him, half of his attitude would be obscured because the reader would have decided that one half was 'right', and given it automatic precedence over the other. This would ruin the balance of the poem, and of the characterisation.

A similar tact is needed in assessing the meaning of 'A Grammarian's Funeral', but this poem is more complicated because the only account we have of the Grammarian is given by one of his admiring students. The speaker naturally sings the praises of his dead master, but is so uncritical in his admiration that he doesn't realise the bathos of the picture he is painting:

Learned we found him!
Yea, but we found him bald too – eyes like lead,
Accents uncertain ...

Strangely enough, though this uncritical admiration may be absurd, the devotion of the Grammarian himself to the pettiest details of his trade emerges with a kind of dignity. In this case, it is not so much the character and taste of the speaker himself as of his master which provide the material of the poem; but even here, Browning has given the speaker sufficient clarity of character in his own right for the reader to make an intelligent assessment of the things he says. For instance, since he is incapable of criticising the Grammarian, the reader must read the praises with an eye for what is *not* said; since the speaker's ideals reach no higher than his master, his account of his master's ideals will probably fall short of the Grammarian's own view of them. But the poor old Grammarian is dead – and his pupil is ultimately as incapable of expressing the truth about him (as he saw it) as is his inscrutable 'enclitic *De*' itself. Like all the other characters in this category, his taste must be extinguished with his death.

'Protus' and 'Instans Tyrannus' both concern themselves with the taste of their speakers, and the result is a curious pair of poems, because far more overtly important issues are also raised in them. In 'Protus', the speaker shares the poem with a verbatim account of what his guidebook says about the child-emperor Protus, and his successor, John the Pannonian. The result is two completely different styles of emperor, seen through the preference of the speaker. The speaker's somewhat sentimental view of Protus forms an ironic window on the ancient world which the baby 'ruled', and the absurdity of absolute power is made plain. On the other hand, the speaker's detestation of the brutal John is counteracted by the annotator in the guidebook, so that once again the speaker's reaction to the grim bust of John is shown as expressing more of his own character than his ability to grasp the power-struggles of the ancients. The poem is a rather comical cameo, portraying a typical genteel tourist, with his guidebook, who has no real understanding of the objects he is looking at, and basically does no more than say, 'I know what I like.' The tyrant in 'Instans Tyrannus' finds his likes and dislikes more troublesome, however: his 'greatness', even though it stoops to being annoyed at one of his lowest subjects, cannot cope with the other's identity. And since all the speaker here believes in is power, it is finally quite appropriate that the poor subject whom he persecutes should invoke the only greater power against him, that of God. The irony lies in the speaker's being intimidated by this, though his humble subject was not intimidated by him. Again the basis of these two poems is really an assertion of personality on the part of the speaker, which is made in terms of 'I like' or 'I dislike' – that is, of taste. In this way, both poems maintain an oddly amoral air, even though the speaker in 'Instans Tyrannus' is obviously a wicked man. The point of the poem is not how evil he is, but how hopelessly enslaved by his own likes and dislikes.

In the poems placed under the heading *Faith*, however, there is considerable moral exploration and it is entirely useful for the reader to consider whether he agrees with the speaker or not, provided that is not all he considers. In 'Saul' and 'An Epistle of Karshish', especially, we find that the speakers confront problems which shake them to the roots of their moral being, and both finally achieve a knowledge of what they really do believe – David in a God with a human face, and Karshish in a kind of spiritual doctoring which can resurrect the dead. These are very profound issues, and any rational discussion of them must surely stir the moral consciousness of the reader. The deliberate preaching of 'The Twins' is much less effective. The nightmarish quest of Childe Roland is clearly imbued with a strong sense of evil, but even so we are never in a position to judge the moral status of the speaker. The fact that the hideous landscape he encounters seems to him to embody evil does not necessarily guarantee that he himself is virtuous. But his moral engagement with his present and past has led to the poem being treated as an allegory by many critics, even though Browning denied that he intended any particular allegorical meaning in the poem. At the end of the poem we are still unsure whether there is a real triumph or just relief that 'some end should be'. The poem does seem to be about faith; not any particular kind of faith, but the grim necessity of continuing in one's beliefs in spite of failure and doubt – Roland, being the ploddingly determined character that he is, has no choice. This does not make him really heroic. The kind of admiration Roland inspires is not such as to cause emulation! Rather, the reader thinks that he has not done too badly, given the appalling terms of his existence. The speaker in 'The Patriot' has in many ways done better, and his faith is more buoyant, whereas the speaker in 'After' has discovered the empty conventionality of what he supposed to be the high ideal of honour. Far more unpleasant is the sophisticated toying with faith of the speaker in 'Before', who is quite prepared to let his friend be killed for a moral gesture, and refers the whole issue to God in a distressingly glib way. In these two poems, Browning has deliberately given us no information at all about the cause of the duel, so that again we are not really in a position to judge the issue.

Our response is required to deal with the involvement of the speaker, and if we judge, it is him we judge.

Both 'The Heretic's Tragedy' and 'Holy-Cross Day' have been placed in the *Faith* group for the purpose of discussion, to emphasise that even where he is writing about moral issues Browning can be comical. He hardly means the reader to regard the 'tragedy' of the heretic burned as being like a normal tragedy on stage. The form of the poem is based on the farcical interludes written in the sixteenth and seventeenth centuries, and the heartless enthusiasm of the speakers hardly puts the reader in a tragic frame of mind. 'Holy-Cross Day' is also overtly comical and verges on the grotesque, yet the issues raised by both poems are serious and concern the nature of faith itself. They reflect the inhumanity which mere moral certainty can inspire, and as in the rest of the poems in *Men and Women*, these bizarre episodes also show Browning's unerringly sharp eye for complacency in all its forms.

The remaining group of poems, which is arguably the most characteristic of Browning himself, comprises those concerned with painting, music and poetry. In a letter of 24 February 1853 to his friend, Joseph Milsand, Browning wrote that he was writing 'lyrics with more music and painting in them than before, so as to get people to hear and see more'. * This aim is undidactic, and his poems on art often discuss style and technique above meaning as such, while both are seen in terms of character. Critics have traditionally claimed that there is a lot of Browning's own philosophy in 'Fra Lippo Lippi', but on the other hand there is the peculiarly sentimental 'Guardian-Angel' where Browning is most unsuccessful at putting himself into a poem (see the notes on this poem in Part 2). 'Memorabilia' is based on an incident in Browning's own life, too, though here the characterisation is much more effective.

In this group, as in the others, it will be helpful for you to put poems together for comparison and contrast, rather than just to try to examine the whole lot in a general way. An obvious pair of poems is 'Andrea del Sarto' and 'Fra Lippo Lippi', which are complementary portraits of aesthetic temperament (melancholy and sanguinary – or pessimistic and optimistic, a little reminiscent of the English epic poet John Milton's (1608–74) 'L'Allegro' and 'Il Penseroso'). Where Lippo is outgoing and gregarious by nature, Sarto is introspective and melancholic, and Browning makes these characteristics the basis of their contrasting philosophies of art. By placing the two poems together, the reader will realise that, even though Lippo's lively appreciation of real life and his commitment to painting it realistically are most attractive qualities, Lippo would not be able to admit, as Andrea does, the 'soul' of a Raphael which transcends the mere realistic technique. Thus the reader

* The letter is published in *Revue Germanique* XII, 1921, p.251.

will have to notice that Browning is not 'for'or *pro* Lippo and 'against' or *anti* Sarto, but sees that both their achievements are unique and serve to make known the general truth of the significance of art itself.

It is in some ways equally illuminating to put 'Cleon' along with 'Andrea del Sarto' for comparison. Both of these artists feel secure in their artistic achievements but totally insecure in their personalities. The aged Cleon cannot overcome his desire for passionate life – refine away on his art though he will, he is still stirred as a man by the beauty of the white slave-girl. He even resents the thought that, when he, the living man, is dead ashes, the works which sprang from his passion for life will go on 'living' to mock him. In Andrea a similar failure is noticeable, though it is not his works which he resents. It is his own mistakes. His stealing from King Francis, his marriage, his final consent to his wife's obvious adultery – in all these he recognises that the same weaknesses of character are reflected in the placid 'greyness' of his painting. In the struggle to 'perfect' their art, they have both become alienated from their real sources of inspiration.

The two poems on music, 'A Toccata of Galuppi's' and 'Master Hugues of Saxe-Gotha', provide an obvious pair for comparison, but either of them could equally well be placed alongside another poem about the interpretation rather than the creation of art, such as 'Old Pictures in Florence' or 'How it Strikes a Contemporary'. For instance, the poor organist who toils his way through Hugues's fugues is not dissimilar in temperament from the would-be connoisseur of 'Old Pictures': both are passionately involved with the works they study and feel betrayed by the very genius they love when they finally realise their own inability to come to terms with the works. Both are almost angry with their heroes. Or again, the scientist who speaks in 'A Toccata of Galuppi's' has a certain amount in common with the speaker in 'How it Strikes a Contemporary': both have become more deeply engaged imaginatively with the inscrutable figures of the artists than they can well account for. Both search the evidence they have, trying to focus a man they can understand within it, and both are of course baffled. Galuppi's music tells the speaker much about eighteenth-century Venice but little of the cynically observant man who composed it: the Spaniard equally is forced to imagine a personality for the poet because the ordinariness of his real appearance does not satisfy him. Both artists seem like spies on their own times to the speakers.

These are not by any means the only useful kinds of comparison. All the poems will illuminate each other. 'Popularity' provides a splendid comparison with 'How it Strikes a Contemporary', as both the speakers are trying to give a picture of a poet; and the argument about style in 'Transcendentalism' can provide new light on Lippo's exclusively realistic philosophy. However, overall it is probably true to say that this group of poems displays a concern with the problem of artistic representation in all its forms and that Browning is basically convinced that the more accurate or realistic the representation, the more effective is the art. The stylised or generalised kinds of art seem to him less capable of 'speaking truth', since truth is finally inseparable from the details of knowledge which make it up.

Men and Women in the Victorian context

In a letter to a friend four years before she met Browning, Elizabeth Barrett wrote of Browning's poetry: 'There are fine things in it – and the presence of genius, never to be denied! At the same time it is hard . . . to *understand* – isn't it? Too hard? I think so!' With her usual expressiveness, Elizabeth Barrett put the opinion of many contemporary readers of Browning's poetry. Her problem was probably not in the form of the dramatic monologue itself, which may perhaps trouble modern readers, as the form was common enough. She herself used it, for instance in 'Lady Geraldine's Courtship' where the speaker is a male poet and lover, and therefore entitled to use such poeticisms as:

When a sudden silver speaking, gravely-cadenced, over-rang them,
And a sudden silken stirring touched my inner nature through . . .

This kind of language actually characterises no-one, but allows the poet to cast herself into a different role for the purposes of the poem. On the other hand, the dramatic monologue was also used for caricature, as in the comical poems of Thomas Hood, for instance in 'The Cigar':

The ardent flame of love
My bosom cannot char,
I smoke, but do not burn
So I have my cigar.

But such comparatively simple uses of the form could hardly have prepared the reading public for the radical way in which Browning used it. Tennyson, too, was beginning to find complexities in the form which were suited to the gloomy doubts of his nature, and it is of some significance that, on the eve of the publication of *Men and Women* in 1855, Tennyson had himself just published his finest dramatic monologue, *Maud*. In this long poem, the speaker, who is melancholic to the point of insanity, tells the story of his ill-fated love in a series of ravishingly beautiful lyrics, each one of which encapsulates and makes music out of a particular mood. Ultimately the character of the speaker does not emerge very clearly, in marked contrast with even the briefest poem in *Men and Women*, but Tennyson considered that the 'moods' of the speaker would be the equivalent in this 'Monodrama' of the several characters usually present in a drama. His conception of the monologue was dramatic, as was Browning's, though with very different consequences in his work. Tennyson's work, however, proved to be considerably more to the taste of Victorian readers than Browning's, as the effect of all the 'mood-music' of Tennyson's lyrics encouraged the reader to empathise with the speaker to some extent. In Browning's monologues, on the other hand, the cool, distancing, ironical technique by which the writer seems to allow the speaker to expose himself more and more as the poem proceeds, perplexed his readers then as it does now.

In Tennyson's *Maud*, the speaker may be insane, but the reader is not expected to doubt that the love he feels is in itself virtuous, a good thing, admirable in its way and capable of raising the poor melancholic who feels it to greater nobility. (The tensions which this assumption sets up within *Maud* actually make it one of the most extraordinary and magnificent poems of the nineteenth century.) Browning's lovers, on the other hand, did not seem on the whole to be improved by love: if they were already selfish, their loving too was selfish; if unconfident, that too was reflected, and so on. The unfamiliar emphasis which Browning placed on characterisation as such led to his being considered a writer of 'grotesque' pieces. Many of the characters were evidently rather wicked, but the undisguised interest which Browning took in them and the fact that he made them discuss high ideals and noble sentiments even while they revealed their own turpitude, baffled his readers then as it may now.

Nevertheless, Browning did win some discerning friends with his poems. The Pre-Raphaelite painter and poet, Dante Gabriel Rossetti, had been an enthusiastic admirer of Browning's poetry from *Sordello* on, and was delighted with *Men and Women*. His patron, John Ruskin (1819–1900), was also impressed, and the novelist George Eliot (1819–80) wrote a generous review. But even so, the reception the poems received disappointed Browning – and Elizabeth Barrett Browning wrote indignantly to a friend that in England only a small group of 'Pre-Raphaelite men' appreciated her husband's new work.

It may be easier for us now to appreciate both Browning's originality and the many strongly Victorian qualities of his work. In this second category must come his intense preoccupation with lyric form, which is so well demonstrated by the wealth of stanza-forms and metres in *Men and Women*. Victorian poets often had an intense interest in prosody, and we find not only Browning but Tennyson and later Gerard Manley Hopkins (1844–89) experimenting with rhyme and metre. Browning and Tennyson even took part in little 'competitions' to see who could find rhymes for such impossible words as 'hippopotamus'. Browning, Tennyson, Matthew Arnold (1822–88) and Arthur Hugh Clough (1819–61) were all lovers of Latin and Greek literature, and this had a marked effect not only on their subject-matter but also on the purely technical aspects of their work.

Another feature of Victorian poetry is its interest in medieval and early Renaissance subjects, and its revival of certain chivalric ideas. We find both of these represented in *Men and Women*. Here it may be illuminating to compare a well-known poem of Tennyson's, 'The Lady of Shallot', with the most overtly chivalric poem in *Men and Women*, 'Childe Roland to the Dark Tower Came'.

In both poems we find a strict verse-form, but in 'The Lady of Shallot', the ballad-like form with its refrain is obviously intended by Tennyson to lend an air of ancient simplicity of heart to the events, which are narrated by an impersonal poetic voice in decorative rather than sentimental fashion. The mere apprehension of Lancelot's chivalrous charms – the flash of his armour, the sweetness of his song – is enough to give rise to Love and so to tragedy. The whole poem is deliberately ornamented like a tapestry, with the detailed landscape, the mirror reflecting the scene outside the window, and the touch of autumn (the reapers are at work in the second stanza) in the east wind as the Lady comes out into the real world for the first and last time. 'Childe Roland' however, vigorously sets out to give the reader the moral intensity of the chivalric quest, but never pauses to mention the flash of armour or the knight's accomplishment as singer, lover, or poet. Browning is less interested in the 'image' of the knight than in trying to imagine what it must have felt like to be one. In order to do this, he has to create a clear, particular speaker whose disillusioned eye perceives a broken, evil landscape all around. Yet in a certain very plain sense, both Browning and Tennyson are following the same trend of interest in the chivalric idea which also inspired much Pre-Raphaelite painting or the fake tournaments with armour and lances and horses which were popular in the mid-century.

There was also an intense interest in what we might today call psychology, or state of mind, shown by Victorian poets. In Tennyson there is a deliberate concentration on mood, leading to the remarkable intensity of language for which he is famous. In Arnold, the reflections are more intellectual but usually based on a particular mood. His loveliest poem, 'Dover Beach', is a fine example of calm despair, and his dramatic poem 'Empedocles on Etna', which Browning admired, creates a mood of violent despair. And the fascination of Hopkins's poetry surely lies in its searing intensity of mental pain, far above even the spiritual questions which are raised by him. Rossetti, too, is fascinated by states of mind, and like the other poets mentioned, seeks to explore them in vividly subjective language. Again, both the contrast with and the similarity to Browning's work should be plain: he shares the interest in mental states, but objectifies them, analyses them in terms of character and situation, instead of trying in a more Romantic way to feel them through his own personality. In this sense, Browning's originality can best be defined in the context of his own time, since the ground he shares with his contemporaries can serve as a foil to his uniqueness.

Part 4

Hints for study

Selecting key poems

You cannot write a good answer on any poetry *without detailed knowledge of the text*. However, since the poems in *Men and Women* are so numerous and so varied, you will have to select some representative ones to study in full detail. The selection you make will depend on your own reading of the poems, but you should know at least five of the major monologues in depth, or more if you choose shorter poems. A good selection should include poems on several related themes. For example, if you were going to write about Browning's handling of moral ideas, you might select as key poems:

1. An Epistle of Karshish } on the nature of God's relation
2. Saul } with mankind

3. 'Childe Roland' } two different angles on the nature
4. Bishop Blougram's Apology } of faith

5. Cleon } contrasting views of the limits of
6. Fra Lippo Lippi } humanism

A good candidate might well be able to show knowledge of other poems, even though he used the key poems to make the major points of his argument. For instance, he might mention the sudden expansion of awareness in the speaker of 'In a Year' – 'What comes next? Is it God?' – as a contrast with the steady contemplation of this question in 'An Epistle of Karshish' or 'Saul'.

Another selection of poems could provide an equally good, though different basis for discussion of the same subject. The student might take as his key poems:

1. Andrea del Sarto } two examinations of failure to live
2. The Statue and the Bust } up to one's ideals and potential

3. A Grammarian's Funeral } ironic studies of wasted lives, not
4. A Toccata of Galuppi's } necessarily to be seen as failures

5. The Last Ride Together } contrasting examples of failures in
6. A Serenade at the Villa } love

An essay based on these poems would place a different connotation on the word 'moral'; instead of concerning man's relation to God, it would be construed in a more humanistic way, as concerning man's relations to other men and himself. Both interpretations could be valid in the context of *Men and Women*.

You could also select your poems on more specific grounds, if you wished. Some themes might be: Browning's handling of ideas about Art (music, painting, poetry) – 'Fra Lippo Lippi' and 'Andrea del Sarto', 'Master Hugues of Saxe-Gotha', 'Popularity' and 'One Word More'; Browning's lovers – 'Mesmerism', 'A Lover's Quarrel', 'By the Fireside', 'In a Balcony' and 'Two in the Campagna'; Browning's use of contrast, as in the pairs of poems and also in a more general sense throughout the work; Browning's method of conveying character by means of rhetorical self-revelation – 'Andrea del Sarto', 'Bishop Blougram's Apology', 'Evelyn Hope', 'De Gustibus—' and 'Instans Tyrannus'.

The areas for study are indeed manifold, and you should follow your own interests as intelligently as possible, rather than using those above which are only given as examples.

Selecting quotations

How to use the texts you have selected is the next problem. This is where your detailed knowledge will stand you in good stead, because you will have the material to hand to answer whatever question you are asked. You should try to remember some quotations, but be careful how you choose them. Go for crucial and characteristic utterances. Your own good sense should indicate these to you – imagine which parts of the speaker's words would strike his listener (and you) most. For instance, Bishop Blougram's comment 'we call the chessboard black, we call it white' not only clinches his argument about human ideas of good and evil, it also suggests to the listener that he himself cannot see a real distinction between good and evil – he equivocates. Thus the listener at this point is not only struck by the Bishop's logic (what he thinks he is demonstrating) but also by the involuntary revelation of his own character, confirming our sense that the choice he made of the Church for his career was an aesthetic and ambitious one, rather than an altruistic or moralistic one. Similarly, Andrea del Sarto's comment that his 'virgin was his wife' reveals far more to the reader than he intended to say about his relations with her.

The quotations you select should be full of meat, so that you can discuss them and not just put them in as mere illustrations. The summaries of the poems in Part 2 of these Notes should help you to choose useful quotations.

Planning your answer

You should always plan your answer to some extent before you start to write it. A simple plan is often best, and you should put down which poems you are going to use and roughly what you are going to say about them at this stage. For instance, if you were faced with the old criticism that Browning's poetry is obscure, you could start planning your answer like this:

'One central meaning seen only by reflexion in details' (Browning in a letter, 1863) – that is, the 'meaning' is never stated except by the details of the monologue itself. Example: 'Memorabilia' – last line 'I forget the rest' implies that no other explanation of the meaning of the feather and the incident of the man who met Shelley is required. So meaning is to be seen in terms of character and situation, or in 'dramatic' terms, as Browning put its.

Now bring in your major poems, showing how all the details add up to a clear picture. In this discussion it would be worth mentioning why you think the poems *might* seem obscure – for instance, that as Browning never tells the reader overtly what he thinks of the speaker, it is hard to agree or disagree with him. You could explain, however, that this 'obscurity' disappears when the reader begins to concentrate on the character of the speaker. Once he does this (which you are showing you have done in your detailed discussion of the poems) the question of whether the character is good or evil, right or wrong, becomes only one among a whole number of more humane questions which the poems answer clearly.

It is the glory and the good of Art
That Art remains the one way possible
Of speaking truth, to mouths like mine at least.

(*The Ring and the Book*)

And by this time, you should be able to conclude that Browning's poems seem 'obscure' only because their method of 'speaking truth' is unfamiliar and original; but that when their 'Art' is analysed, their meaning and 'truth' emerges clearly.

This question, incidentally, is dealt with in a more abstract but also more profound way by the English poet and critic Algernon Charles Swinburne (1837–1909) in his essay on George Chapman (1875).*

You could of course argue that Browning *is* obscure, but in that case your arguments would be different. The method of planning could be similar, however.

---

* Included in J. R. Watson (ed.), *Browning's 'Men and Women' and Other Poems*, 1974, pp.61–5.

Specimen questions

Here are some questions for you to try, so that you get used to organising your knowledge to form an answer. The simpler questions are put first.

(1) Do you think Browning is an optimist? Show detailed knowledge of at least four poems in your answer.

(2) 'Manners make men'. Do you think Browning would agree?

(3) How does Browning use the form of the dramatic monologue?

(4) Do you consider *Men and Women* achieves poetic greatness as a whole, or do you think it has a few great poems in it?

(5) By close reference to at least four poems, show how Browning uses rhyme and metre to achieve effects which are comical and ironic.

(6) What are Browning's characteristics as a love poet?

(7) Do you think the poems in *Men and Women* can justifiably be called 'dramatic'?

(8) How does Browning use the principle of contrast in *Men and Women*?

(9) [Browning's] lyric and dramatic writing is apt to be neither dramatic nor lyrical, simply because of the writer's natural and inevitable tendency to analysis, which can only express itself either through the method of direct exposition or in the form of elaborate mental monologue.' (A. C. Swinburne, *Essay on George Chapman*). Do you agree?

(10) The epilogue to 'Bishop Blougram's Apology' says that the Bishop 'said true things, but called them by wrong names'.
Do you feel this could be said about other characters in *Men and Women*? Use at least four poems to illustrate your answer.

(11) In an essay on Browning's style* G. K. Chesterton wrote: 'Browning is a man whose excitement for the glory of the obvious is so great that his speech becomes eccentric through his advocacy of the ordinary, and goes mad for the love of sanity.' Do you agree?

(12) Reviewing *Men and Women* in 1856, George Eliot wrote: 'To read Browning [the reader] must exert himself, but he will exert himself to some purpose. If he finds the meaning difficult of access, it is always worth his effort – if he has to dive deep, "he rises with his pearl" . . .' Do you agree?

* Included in J. R. Watson (ed.), op.cit., pp.75–95.

(13) 'Browning's gift is shown by the way in which he accepts a character, throws it into some situation, or apprehends it in some delicate pause of life, in which for a moment it becomes ideal.' Discuss this idea of Walter Pater's.

(14) 'Browning conveys his doctrine not as such but as an enthusiasm of living' (Edward Dowden, *Life of Robert Browning*). Discuss.

Specimen answers

'The dramatic monologue ... requires sympathy for the speaker as a condition of reading the poem' (Robert Langbaum, *The Poetry of Experience*). Discuss this assertion in relation to your reading of Browning's *Men and Women*.

The monologues in *Men and Women* are so varied that they require a far more varied response from the reader than just that of sympathy for the speakers, though that feeling might well be appropriate in some cases. For instance, the reader's sympathy is certainly enlisted by the speaker in 'Fra Lippo Lippi', and by the completely different one in 'By the Fire-side'. Fra Lippo Lippi is intent upon gaining the sympathy of his hearers so that they will not arrest him, and he flatters them and tries to amuse them, as well as pleading more overtly for their sympathy:

> You should not take a fellow eight years old
> And make him swear to never kiss the girls.

For different reasons, the speaker in 'By the Fire-side' is also working upon the sympathy of the hearer or reader. He is actually addressing his 'perfect wife', and can rely upon her giving a sympathetic hearing to his attempt to describe the mystery of the moment of their mutual consent to become no longer 'Friends – lovers that might have been', but 'mixed at last/ In spite of the mortal screen'. Here the intensely personal nature of the revelation that the character is describing enlists the reader's sympathy even though he is not the person addressed, and the poem is moving because of this.

However, in most of the monologues it seems that the speaker does not rely upon the reader's sympathy, and not just because he/she may not be appealing for sympathy from the person addressed in the poem. In most of the poems, the 'condition for reading' would be a close and critical attention to the details of what the speaker is saying, and only when that has been given is the reader really in a position to know what the poem is about. For instance, the speaker in 'A Epistle of Karshish' is neither particularly sympathetic nor unsympathetic as a character. His major claim upon the reader's interest is the intensity of his commitment to doctoring. The poem is deliberately 'relating the strange *medical* experience', and if anything, the specific slant which this speaker professionally gives to his whole account serves to distinguish him from the reader (assuming the reader is not necessarily a doctor, even though the addressee, Abib, is). The interest of the poem lies primarily in the speaker's objectivity to the reader, and coincidentally in the ideas he raises which are of universal human interest. However, Browning's method enables him to discuss these ideas with passion and energy, not from his own standpoint but from the imaginary one of his character. If the reader merely offered a basic human sympathy with the character, the point of his method would be lost, since it consists in distinguishing the truth or falsity of the character's ideas in relative terms, and only in detail, and not in the generally egocentric sense implied in the question. Browning himself wrote that his work is 'meant to have one central meaning, seen only by reflexion in details'.

A close examination of 'Karshish' will show this to be the case. Whereas it might genuinely be possible for the reader to 'sympathise' with Karshish's excitement at the assertion Lazarus makes that his healer was 'God himself,/Creator and sustainer of the world,/That came and dwelt in flesh on it a while!', the next minute Karshish's comment is so narrowly medical as to preclude our 'sympathy':

Why write of trivial matters, things of price
Calling at every moment for remark?
I noticed on the margin of a pool
Blue-flowering borage ...

Surely most readers could not really sympathise with Karshish's estimate that borage is a more important subject than Lazarus's story? In fact, in spite of himself, Karshish too finds Lazarus's claims fascinating, but unlike most of the readers, he cannot finally see the miracle as anything but superior medicine, and this is where the great strength of the poem lies. His definite and alien reflections on a story which Christians would take for granted as part of their own mythology provide a radical exploration of its human importance, not its place in the dogma. The breadth of Browning's vision and method here goes far beyond what could be achieved merely by feeling sympathetic even to a nice doctor like Karshish.

But the claim that 'sympathy for the speaker' is the basis of the reader's response to the dramatic monologues in *Men and Women* is even more inappropriate when applied to poems where the speaker's character itself is being held up for ironic scrutiny. This is plainly the case in 'Instans Tyrranus' or 'Bishop Blougram's Apology', where the speakers' assumptions of their own superiority over their listeners make them reveal their most unsympathetic qualities, and it could also be argued that it is the case with 'Andrea del Sarto'. In this poem, the speaker is so self-pitying and morally lazy that, even though we might feel some sympathy for his situation (his unfaithful wife, his alienation from the court of Francis where his art was fostered), we find it very hard indeed to sympathise with *him*. His crime in stealing money from Francis is neither here nor there; nor do we even find it terribly shocking that he left his parents to die in poverty: what really makes the reader impatient with Andrea is his peculiar complacency about his own failure. We feel much more passionately than he does, that, if he really had the talent to 'bring the sweat' into Raphael's brow, he would hardly need his wife's encouragement. Yet he luxuriates in the idea, he is charmed to think that Michelangelo noticed his work, and he foolishly judges himself as nearly equal with the great artists, Raphael, Michelangelo and Leonardo da Vinci, blaming his wife for his failure to realise his artistic potential. There is a whining, complacent, dreamy quality about his character which lets us know with certainty that his 'faultless' work is actually not in the same league as Raphael's, even though Raphael may misdraw an arm or two! In this sense, then, the more Andrea says, the more he reveals himself, the less the reader can sympathise with him. The final touch of sending his wife out placidly to her tryst with the cousin completes our sense of a man whose passionless 'silver-grey' spirit could never make his art anything more positive than 'fault*less*'.

Thus, while it is perhaps useful for the reader to sympathise with the speaker in some of the poems, sympathy is very far from being a 'condition for reading' many of the poems in *Men and Women*. The responses of the reader need to be far more sensitively attuned to the different characters than this statement suggests.

The quotation on which this answer is based comes from Robert Langbaum's *The Poetry of Experience*, which gives a romantic reading of Browning's work. Since this is opposite in tendency to the interpretation in these Notes, the student is advised to have a look at this book. The relevant extract can be found in J. R. Watson's *Browning: 'Men and Women' and Other Poems*.

Comment on 'Browning's serious use of the grotesque' (G. K. Chesterton).

There are several aspects of Browning's work, which have been considered 'grotesque', that is to say, distorted or ugly, and in many cases this quality has simply been regretted by the critics. However, even the most bizarre and repulsive aspects of Browning's deliberately grotesque pieces are seriously used by the poet to make his meaning plain. He works upon a principle of contrast, evident in his ironic technique for presenting characters, and if we take this principle into account the 'grotesque' aspects of his poetry will be seen to make a serious contribution to its meaning.

An obvious example of a grotesque vision is to be found in 'The Heretic's Tragedy', where the burning at the stake of Jacques du Bourg-Molay ('John' of the poem) is given to us in graphic and hideous detail. The speaker in the poem adds another element to the grotesque picture because he is actually rejoicing at the horrible scene:

> Then up they hoist me John in a chafe,
>   Sling him fast like a hog to scorch,
> Spit in his face, then leap back safe,
>   Sing 'Laudes' and bid clap-to the torch.

The blithe inhumanity of this attitude lends an air of comedy to the whole proceeding which is truly grotesque. But the poem does not leave it at that: once the fire is lit, the burning figure of the heretic becomes a strangely beautiful thing, compared in brightness to a rose (of Sharon). The speaker does not alter his attitude, but what he describes has an appalling beauty about it which is far grimmer in itself even than the speaker's inhumanity. The last lines of the poem pick up both aspects of this tragedy. The speaker triumphantly says: 'Forth John's soul flared into the dark', but he is answered by the Abbot who reminds us that the same Judgment awaits us all: 'God help all poor souls lost in the dark!' Thus the grotesqueness of the actual scene, and the hideousness of the speaker's attitude, are both used as contrasts with the strange transfiguration of the heretic and the humane reminder of the Abbot's last words which are also part of the same religion that causes the 'tragedy'.

In 'A Grammarian's Funeral', Browning makes a different use of distortion and absurdity, but again makes them contrast with puzzlingly fine qualities. The dead Grammarian is praised by one of his pupils, but in such terms that we feel he has really wasted his life. Quite unselfconsciously, the pupil tells us that the Grammarian '. . . stepped on with pride/Over men's pity' and we see both sides of the case at once. On the one hand, there is something genuinely admirable, noble even, about the severe devotion to his task which motivated the grammarian. But at the same time, we see the pitying looks he inspires in people around him, who consider he is wasting his life. Similarly, even though the speaker enthusiastically embraces 'the doctrine of the enclitic *De*' as if it were an article of faith, the reader is left with a sense of the grotesque misapplication of the fine human qualities to petty ends. In fact, the effect of the contrast is even more skilfully achieved than this implies, because Browning has set the whole scene at the Grammarian's funeral:

the Grammarian cannot speak for himself. The uncritically admiring attitude his pupil expresses actually makes the reader more aware of the irony of such heroic efforts being applied to particles of grammar than he would be if the Grammarian himself were speaking. But for the same reason, the dead man has a claim upon our pity and respect which is not spoiled by his pupil's tactless praises –

Learned we found him.
Yea, but we found him bald too . . .

Here again, the grotesque is used not as an end in itself but as a contrast with admirable qualities, so that the real irony of the poem can make its meaning clear.

Browning, however, is often accused also of using a grotesque kind of language. His rapid, unmellifluous verses are pointed at as evidence that, though he might be a clever thinker, he was not much of a lyricist. Here again, he is making a serious use of grotesque forms of language in order to draw attention to the qualities of the speaker rather than those of the poet. Tennyson's speaker in *Maud* would be a gifted poet if we were to take his verses as evidence, but in fact we do not do this. We allow Tennyson his beauty of language as part of his means of creating his 'monodrama'. Browning also felt that he was not just 'putting on' voices, mimicking the way his characters speak, but that he was actually 'entering' them, as he says in 'One Word More', and endowing their characters and situations with poetry. Thus the speaker in 'Love Among the Ruins' is able to create a unique verse-form which expresses perfectly his relaxed and confident pleasure as he walks to meet his mistress. On the other hand, the quick-tempered changeable metre of the speaker in 'A Lovers' Quarrel' expresses his mood and situation well, too. Even among the blank-verse monologues we find Browning's attention has gone into finding a poetic equivalent of the speakers' moods and dramatic situations rather than into trying to express their ideas mellifluously. Thus, Bishop Blougram's extended metaphor of 'the Outward Bound' gives us the exact measure of his sincerity – he is actually playing with words. Gigadibs's silence, by contrast, becomes almost a sign of a more sincere nature! Fra Lippo Lippi rushes through his words like a nervous comedian, sometimes breaking into snatches of song, because he is intent upon engrossing the attention and winning the sympathy of his captors.

'Tell you, I liked your looks at very first.
Let's sit and set things straight now, hip to haunch.

Thus the very lack of conventionally beautiful language is indicative of Browning's serious intentions in creating his *Men and Women*.

The last use of the grotesque which there is time to mention is

Browning's use of it in its own right, as he does in the nightmarish landscape of 'Childe Roland to the Dark Tower Came'. Here the mood of the speaker is of paramount importance to the poem's meaning, and his despair and self-contempt are reflected brilliantly in his descriptions of the landscape and the hateful cripple who directs him. When Roland turns from the horrible landscape which surrounds him to his own thoughts, he finds these even more grotesque – Cuthbert and Giles, his fellow knights, both appear to him in their dishonour. 'Better this present than a past like that!' he exclaims, but the present offers him horrors which are also mysteries – the circle of beaten ground, the 'shriek' as he fords the river, the uninterpretable 'engine'. In this case, the grotesque images of the poem are used to create an atmosphere of horror and despair, and their grotesqueness is the point.

It can be said, then, that Browning does make serious use of the grotesque in many ways in his poetry. It is an unusually significant element of his aesthetic sense, since he does not simply use the grotesque to achieve gothic effects. As G. K. Chesterton wrote, in the same work* as that in which he coined the phrase which is the topic of this essay: 'he was a very perfect artist, and a particularly perfect artist in the use of the grotesque.'

* G. K. Chesterton, *Robert Browning* (English Men of Letters series), Macmillan, London, 1903, ch. VI.

Part 5

Suggestions for further reading

The Text

Robert Browning: The Poems edited by John Pettigrew, supplemented and completed by Thomas J. Collins, 2 vols, Yale University Press, New Haven, Conn., and London, 1981, and Penguin Books, Harmondsworth, 1981. Volume I contains *Men and Women*. This is the only edition with full notes. It is expensive, but very good. Its information supersedes that given in W. C. DeVane, *A Browning Handbook*, Appleton Century Crofts, New York, 2nd edn, 1955.

Browning: Poetical Works 1833–1864, edited by Ian Jack, Oxford Standard Authors Series, Oxford University Press, Oxford, 1970. This edition has no notes.

Biography

IRVINE, W. and HONAN, P.: *The Ring, the Book and the Poet*, Bodley Head, London, 1975.

Criticism

The following books containing work on different aspects of Browning's poetry by eminent critics are recommended, so that you can see the range of critical attitudes to Browning and choose for yourself what sort of line you prefer to follow.

ARMSTRONG, ISOBEL (ED.): *Writers and their Background: Browning*, Bell, London, 1974. This contains essays on Browning's background and the influences on his work.

DREW, PHILIP (ED.): *Robert Browning: A Collection of Critical Essays*, Methuen, London, 1966.

LANGBAUM, ROBERT: *The Poetry of Experience*, Random House, New York and London, 1957.

LITZINGER, B. and SMALLEY, K. K. (EDS): *Browning, The Critical Heritage*, Routledge, London, 1970. This records the changes in critical attitude towards Browning's works from their first publication.

WATSON, J. R. (ED.): *Browning: 'Men and Women' and Other Poems*, Casebook Series, Macmillan, London, 1974. This includes essays by George Eliot, Swinburne, Henry James, G. K. Chesterton and Robert Langbaum, and two enjoyable parodies of Browning's poetry.

The author of these notes

MARY MONTAUT is a graduate of the Universitities of Cambridge and London and teaches Modern English at University College, Dublin. She has also taught at secondary level, including preparing students for 'A' and 'S' level examinations. Her doctoral thesis is on Robert Browning.

The first 200 titles

		Series number
CHINUA ACHEBE	*A Man of the People*	(116)
	Arrow of God	(92)
	Things Fall Apart	(96)
ELECHI AMADI	*The Concubine*	(139)
JOHN ARDEN	*Serjeant Musgrave's Dance*	(159)
AYI KWEI ARMAH	*The Beautyful Ones Are Not Yet Born*	(154)
JANE AUSTEN	*Emma*	(142)
	Northanger Abbey	(1)
	Persuasion	(69)
	Pride and Prejudice	(62)
	Sense and Sensibility	(91)
SAMUEL BECKETT	*Waiting for Godot*	(115)
SAUL BELLOW	*Henderson, The Rain King*	(146)
ARNOLD BENNETT	*Anna of the Five Towns*	(144)
WILLIAM BLAKE	*Songs of Innocence, Songs of Experience*	(173)
ROBERT BOLT	*A Man For All Seasons*	(51)
CHARLOTTE BRONTË	*Jane Eyre*	(21)
EMILY BRONTË	*Wuthering Heights*	(43)
JOHN BUCHAN	*The Thirty-Nine Steps*	(89)
ALBERT CAMUS	*L'Etranger (The Outsider)*	(46)
GEOFFREY CHAUCER	*Prologue to the Canterbury Tales*	(30)
	The Franklin's Tale	(78)
	The Knight's Tale	(97)
	The Merchant's Tale	(193)
	The Miller's Tale	(192)
	The Nun's Priest's Tale	(16)
	The Pardoner's Tale	(50)
	The Wife of Bath's Tale	(109)
	Troilus and Criseyde	(198)
SAMUEL TAYLOR COLERIDGE	*Selected Poems*	(165)
WILKIE COLLINS	*The Woman in White*	(182)
SIR ARTHUR CONAN DOYLE	*The Hound of the Baskervilles*	(53)
JOSEPH CONRAD	*Heart of Darkness*	(152)
	Lord Jim	(150)
	Nostromo	(68)
	The Secret Agent	(138)
	Youth and Typhoon	(100)
DANIEL DEFOE	*Moll Flanders*	(153)
	Robinson Crusoe	(28)
CHARLES DICKENS	*A Tale of Two Cities*	(70)
	Bleak House	(183)
	David Copperfield	(9)
	Great Expectations	(66)
	Nicholas Nickleby	(161)
	Oliver Twist	(101)
	The Pickwick Papers	(110)
JOHN DONNE	*Selected Poems*	(199)
THEODORE DREISER	*Sister Carrie*	(179)
GEORGE ELIOT	*Adam Bede*	(14)
	Silas Marner	(98)
	The Mill on the Floss	(29)
T. S. ELIOT	*Four Quartets*	(167)
	Murder in the Cathedral	(149)
	Selected Poems	(155)
	The Waste Land	(45)
WILLIAM FAULKNER	*Absalom, Absalom!*	(124)
	As I Lay Dying	(44)
	Go Down, Moses	(163)
	The Sound of the Fury	(136)
HENRY FIELDING	*Joseph Andrews*	(105)
	Tom Jones	(113)
F. SCOTT FITZGERALD	*The Great Gatsby*	(8)
E. M. FORSTER	*A Passage to India*	(151)